The expanded practice of the artist's book

msdm publications

The expanded practice of the artist's book

Immersion in the artist's museum

Francisco Varela

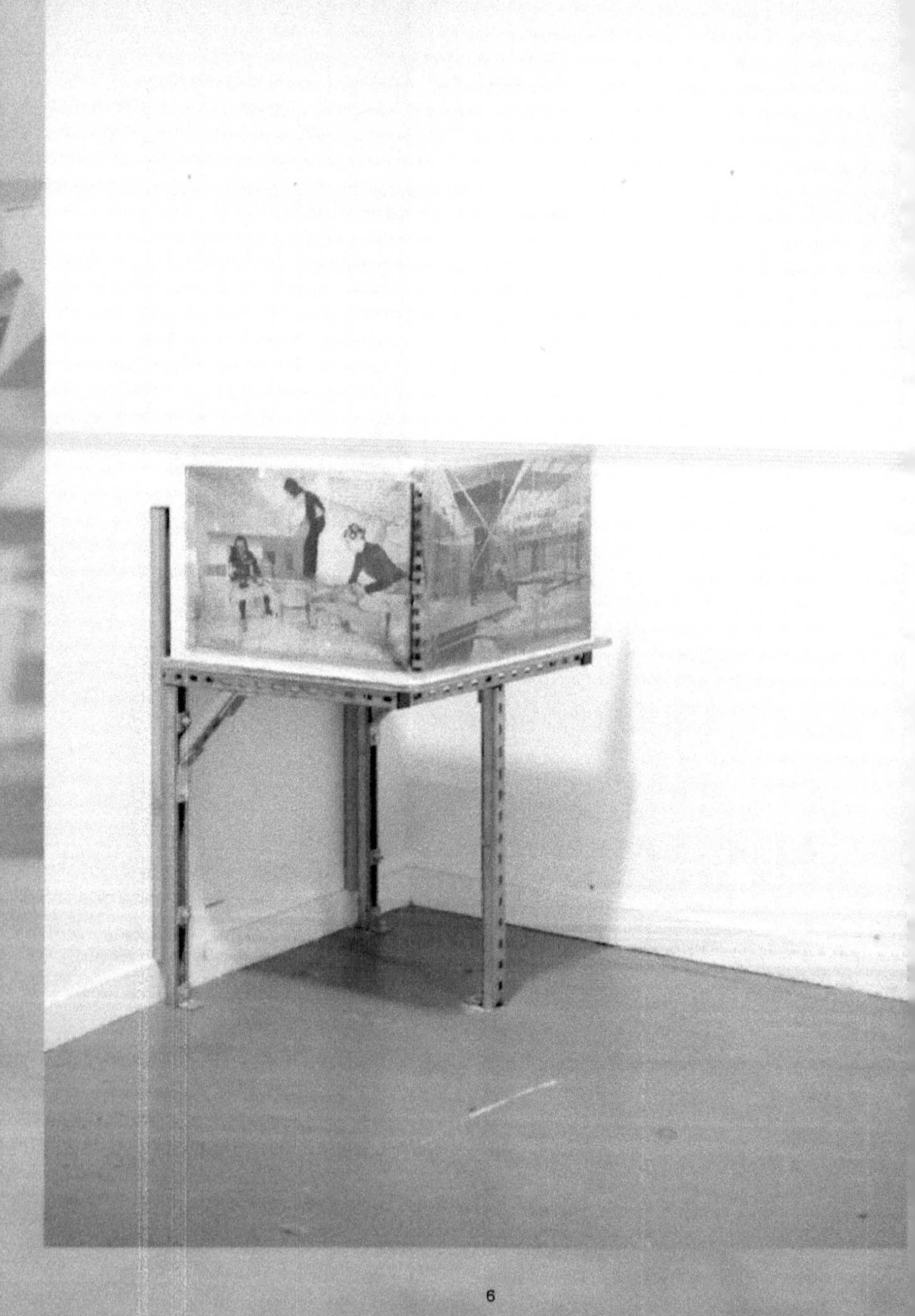

paula roush's artistic practice presents itself as a unique case study of a live–work method and it is the aim of this essay to analyse, contextualize and query the principles that guide this method.

It is an artistic and experiential practice that performs a reinterpretation of the city through collection, research and display of materials as well as an idiosyncratic practice of space making.

In doing so it formulates alternative urban narratives, combining elements of personal biography and urban storytelling.

This is achieved through an immersive practice that results in artefacts, books and in the musealisation of the architectural spaces she occupies.

The first section of the essay explores the 'expanded' characteristics of the artist's book, probing whether this notion is extendable to the activity of space production practiced in the house–studio–gallery, an activity which is unique to and inseparable from the live–work method.

These artistic methodologies are clarified within an interdisciplinary framework that includes the concepts of 'autoethnography,' 'space–time sequence' and 'contemporaneity.'

The second section explores
the notion of 'dispositif,' with
the intention to reveal the
multiple structuring elements of
a live—work practice here called
'immersive.'

The third section analyses the
'museographic' process inherent
to the practice associated with
the house—studio—gallery.
This live—work—curation method
is identified in relation to various
museological frameworks that
are exercised in that space.

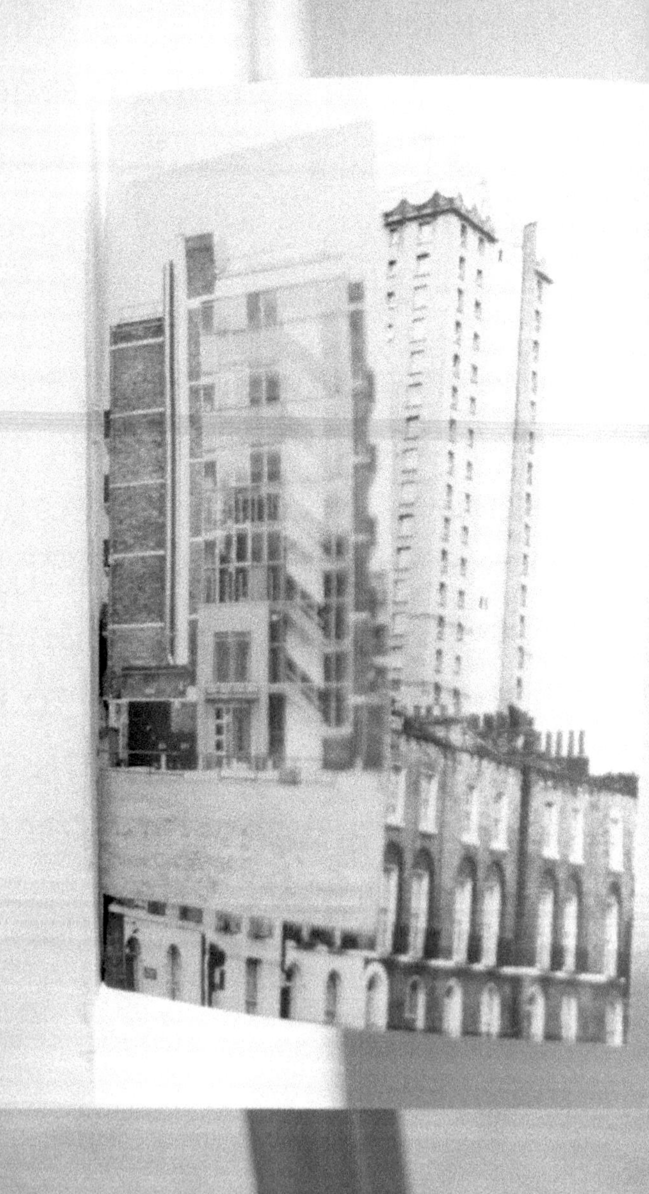

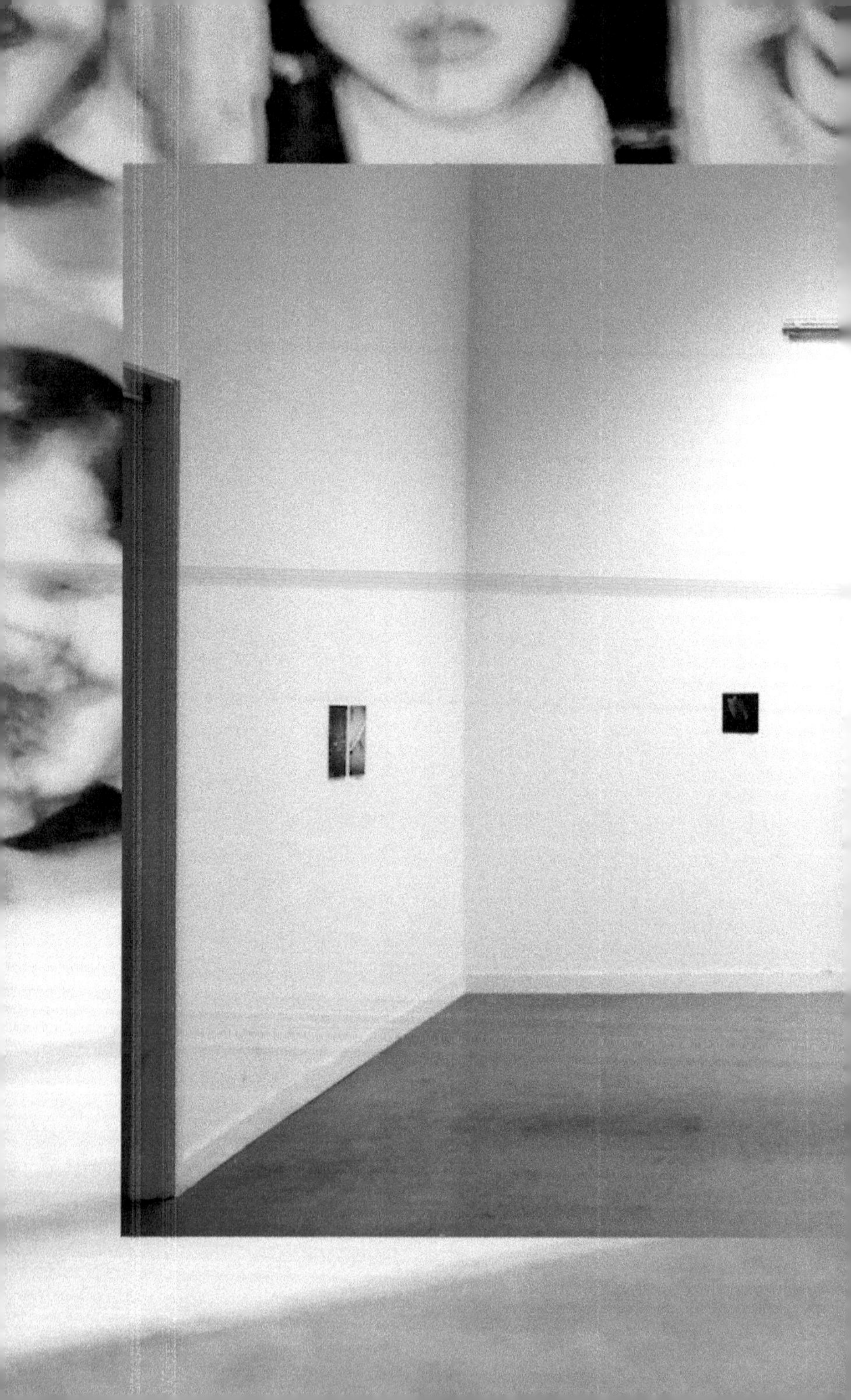

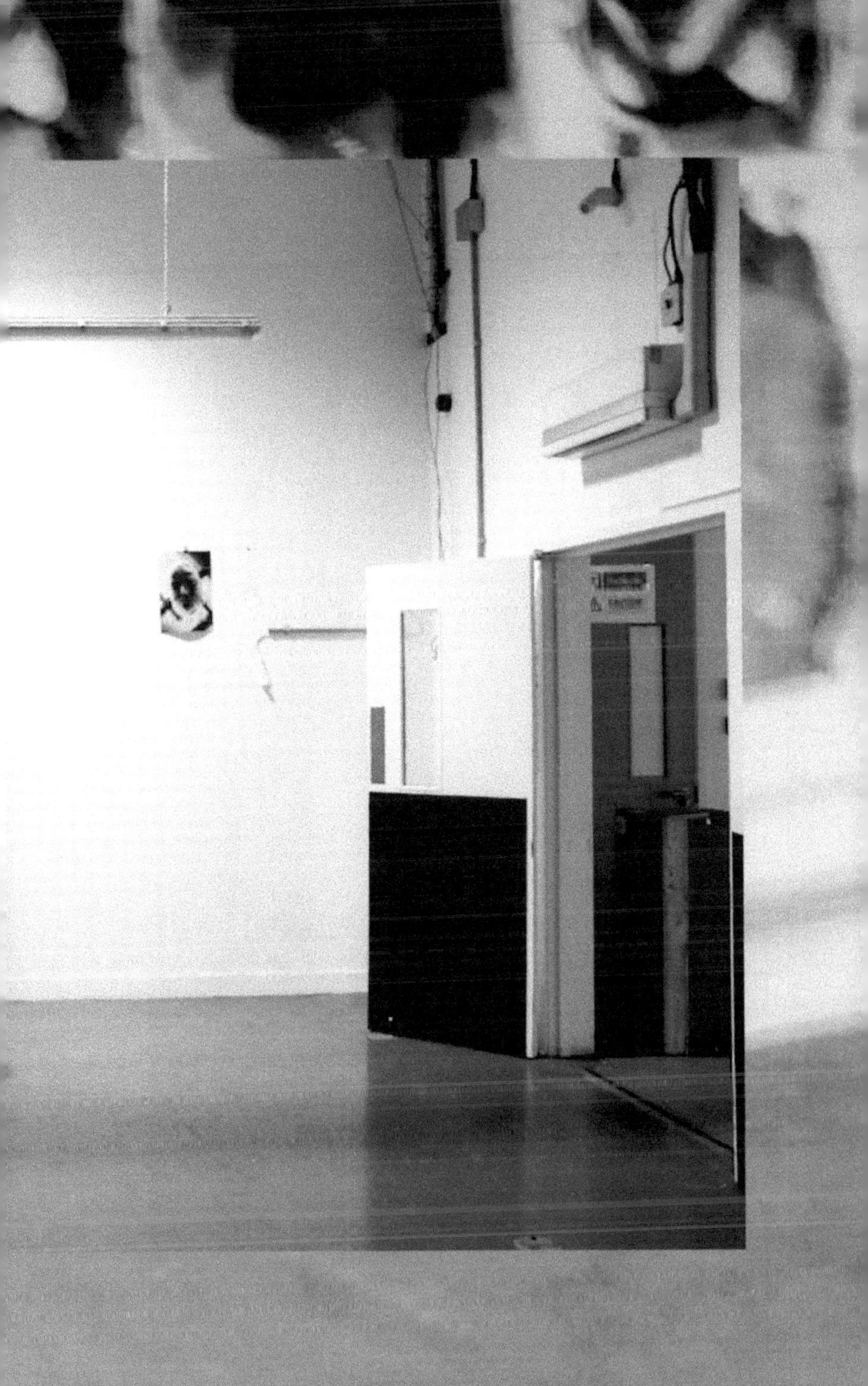

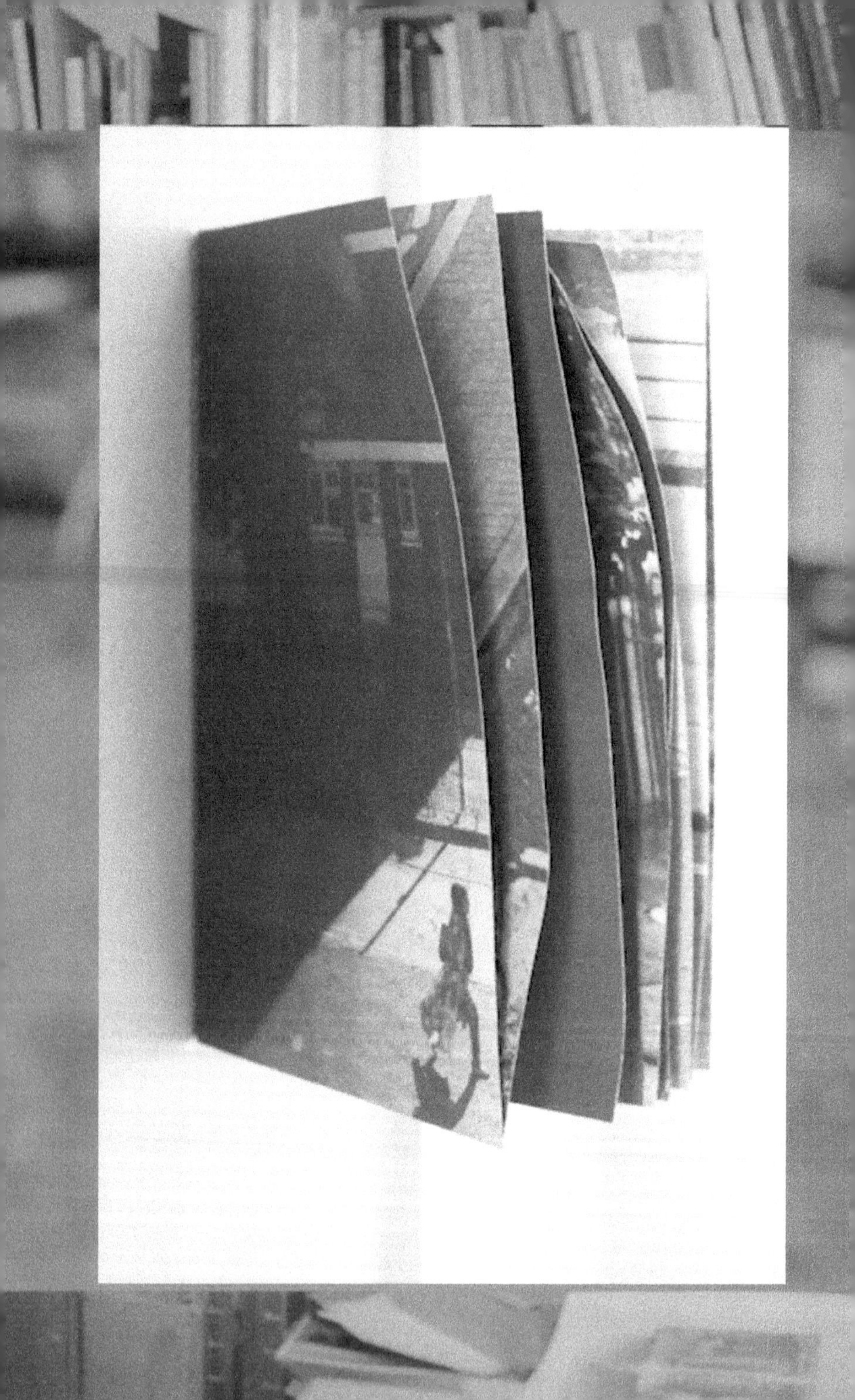

1.
The expanded practice of the artist's book

In this section I reflect on paula's
artistic practice. It is a photographic
practice and takes place in different
formats (or mediums), including
installation and publishing.

For the past five years,
paula has been developing
this practice in spaces that
are simultaneously home,
studio and gallery.
It is pertinent to reflect on this live–
work method as it is
a singular artistic activity,
articulated in a unique way
with the making of artist's books
(which interests me particularly,
since I am also a 'maker'
of artists' books).

My intention with this reflection is to contribute to an understanding of the unique characteristics of the artist's book practice. I am interested in the ways paula's artwork is in its totality anchored in an expanded practice of the artist's book.

These are my initial questions:

Is it possible that the installations (artistic modalities / types of work) produced in these spaces are also books?

How does the spatialisation of the book's components expand its nature and character to the point where it can no longer be considered a book?

Is this combination of 'artistic'
and 'domestic' artefacts, and their
ongoing temporal and narrative
reconfiguration, related to the
typology of the book (in whatever
form we understand it)?

Or do these hybrid artefacts become
other 'things,' autonomous from a
notion of the book?

Is all of this activity informed/
supported in its *modus operandi*
by the making of books?

Is the totality of this live–work space
a book, i.e., a great 'sandwich of
materials,' as Dieter Roth defined
the artist's book?

Is the 'immersive' practice
itself articulated with the
methodologies of creation,
reading and transgression of
the 'expanded' book?

This reflection is based on two
works of different nature and
production process, related to the
period in which I experienced them
and conversations I had with paula
during my visit to her space,[1] in
Woolwich, South–East London.

These works are <u>Blackchapel</u>
and <u>Untitled</u> (working title),
two 'sandwiches of materials'
installed throughout the building.

1 I was in residence at msdm house-studio-gallery November 21–24, 2019.

I investigate whether it is
possible to apply the notion of
'expanded field' to these works,
and relate this to the condition
of 'contemporaneity.'

Finally, I discuss whether
collections and books share
the same condition.

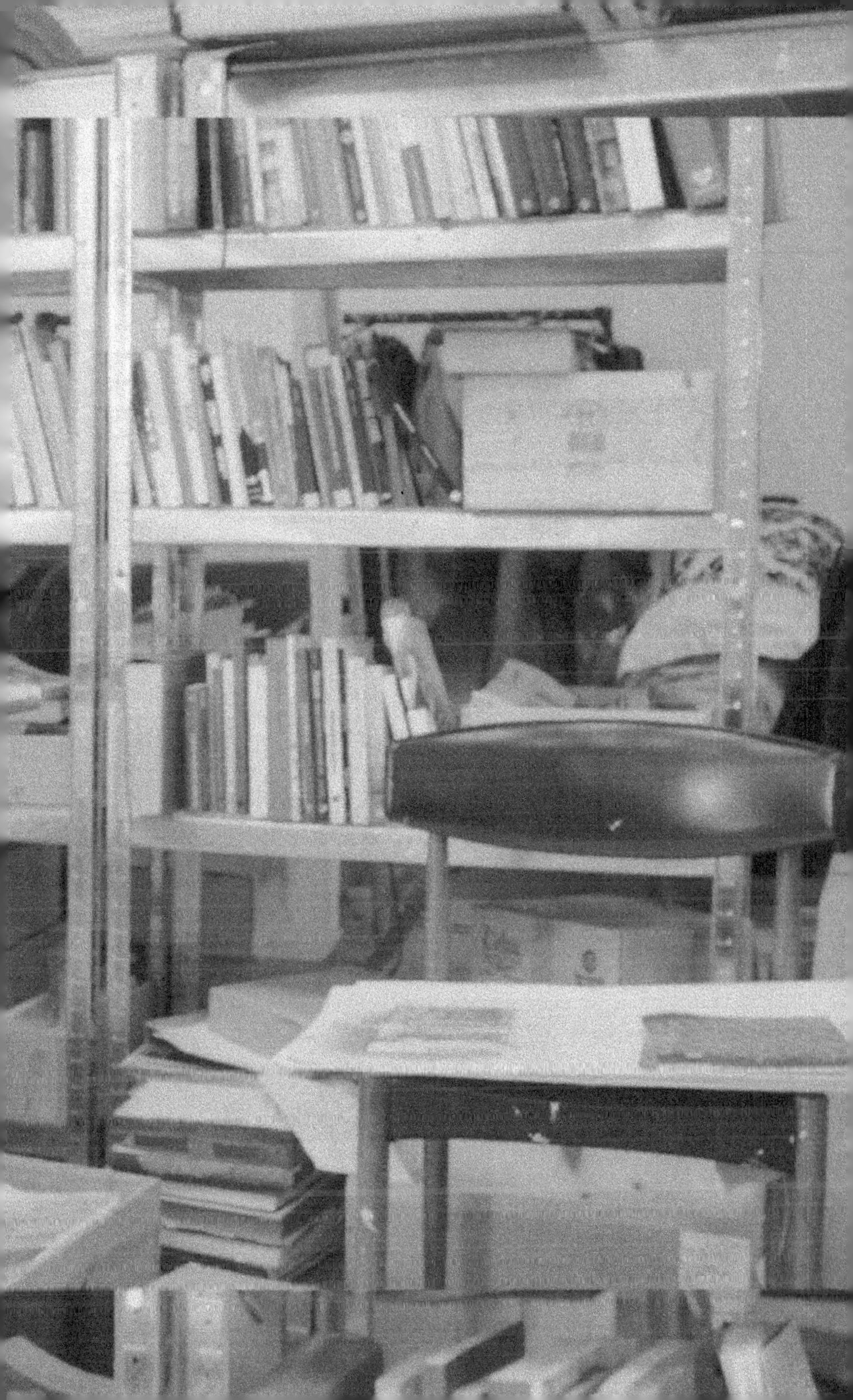

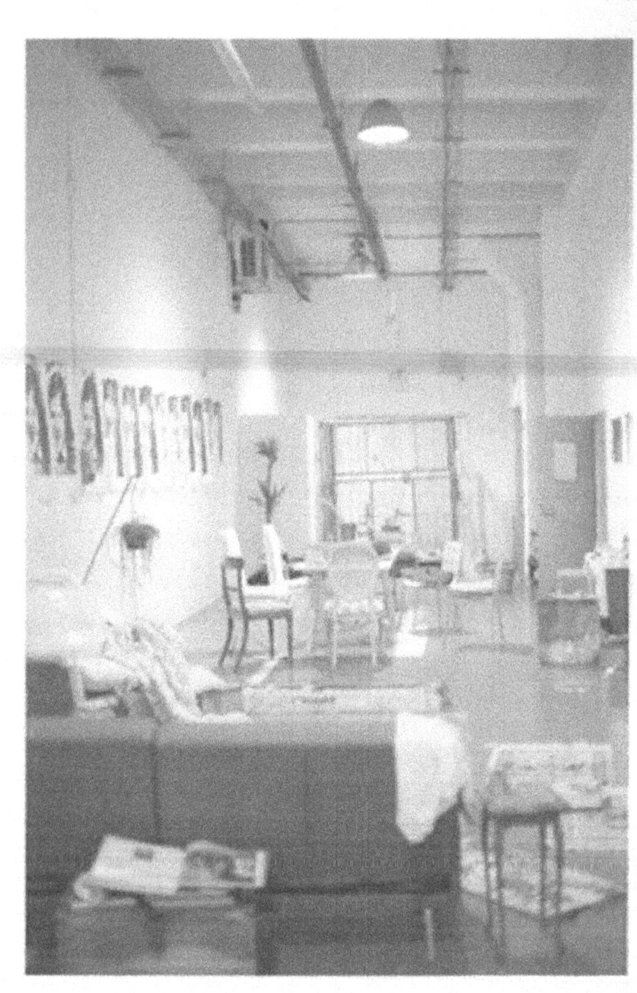

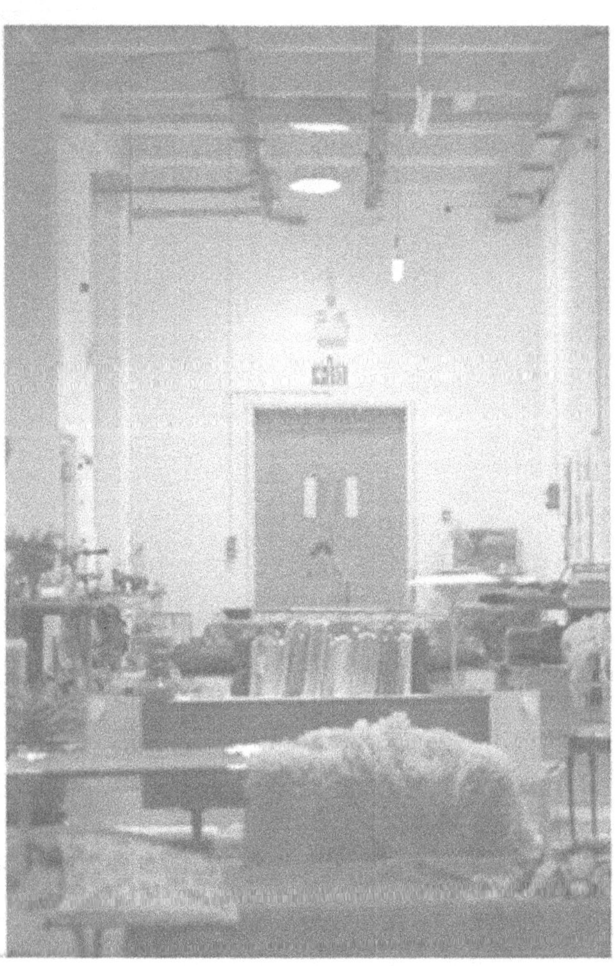

WHITECHAPEL

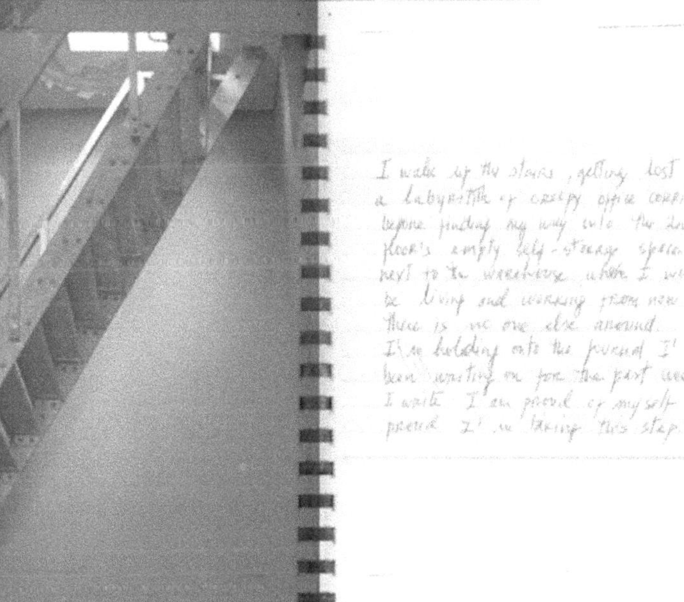

I walk up the stairs, getting lost in
a labyrinth of creepy office corridors
before finding my way into the 2nd
floor's empty self-storage space,
next to the warehouse where I will
be living and working from now on.
There is no one else around.
I'm holding onto the journal I've
been writing on for the past weeks.
I write I am proud of myself,
proud I'm taking this step.

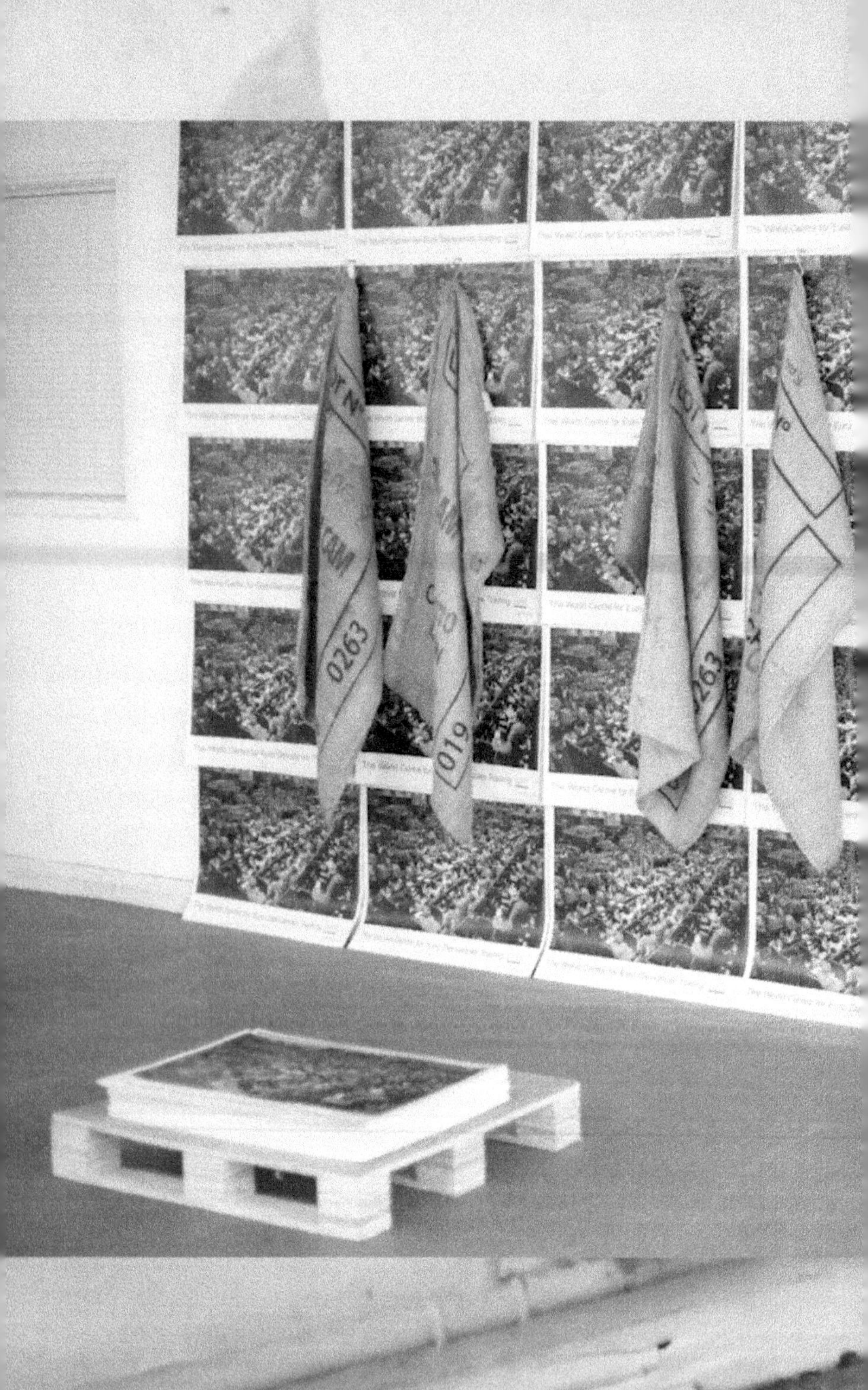

Autoethnography

The field of creation and publication of artists' books has a past that begins with the artistic vanguards in the early 20th century and had its resurgence and theoretical reformulation from the 1960s onwards.[2]

In recent years, the artist 's book has been, for some, the chosen vehicle for expression and exhibition of their work, becoming itself an alternative to the institutional art gallery. Furthermore, it is almost impossible to assign definite boundaries and characteristics

2 See Johanna Drucker, *The Century of Artists' Books* (Michigan: Granary Books, 1995).

to what is considered an
artist's book; it is rather in the
questioning of its limits that an
expanded practice emerges,
that is at the edge (or beyond)
its definition as book.[3]

Instead of an activity exclusively
focused on the making of artist's
books, paula's main concern
is her immersion in the places
where she lives, and sources her
materials from. These materials are
investigated in their context, history,
provenance and relationship to the
community. As well as in relation
to the tripartite use she makes of
the space, where living space is
indistinguishable from studio and
exhibition spaces.

3 As debated, for example, in Leszek Brogowski, Anne Moeglin-Delcroix
  and Aurelie Noury (Eds), *Le livre d'Artiste: Quels Projets Pour L'Art*. Actes
  Du Colloque (Rennes: Incertain Sens, 2013).

This practice and its ethnographic research methodology assume the characteristics of an autoethnography, similar to that outlined by Tony E. Adams, Carolyn Ellis and Stacy Holmes Jones:

> *Autoethnography is a research method that uses personal experience ('auto') to describe and interpret ('graphy') cultural texts, experiences, beliefs, and practices ('ethno'). Autoethnographers believe that personal experience is infused with political / cultural norms and expectations, and they engage in rigorous self reflection — typically referred to as 'reflexivity' — in order to identify*

and interrogate the intersections between the self and social life.[4]

Although the methods of this immersion process vary according to the location of paula's house–studio–gallery, there is always a simultaneous redefinition of her identity. The artefacts created as a result of this process — installations and objects — are transient and exist in a state of permanent mutability.
Books are created before, during and after the making of these installations, sometimes with the materials used in them.

4 Tony E. Adams, Carolyn Ellis and Stacy Holmes Jones, "Autoethnography,"
In *The International Encyclopedia of Communication Research Methods,*
(Hoboken, NJ: John Wiley & Sons, 2017), 1-11.

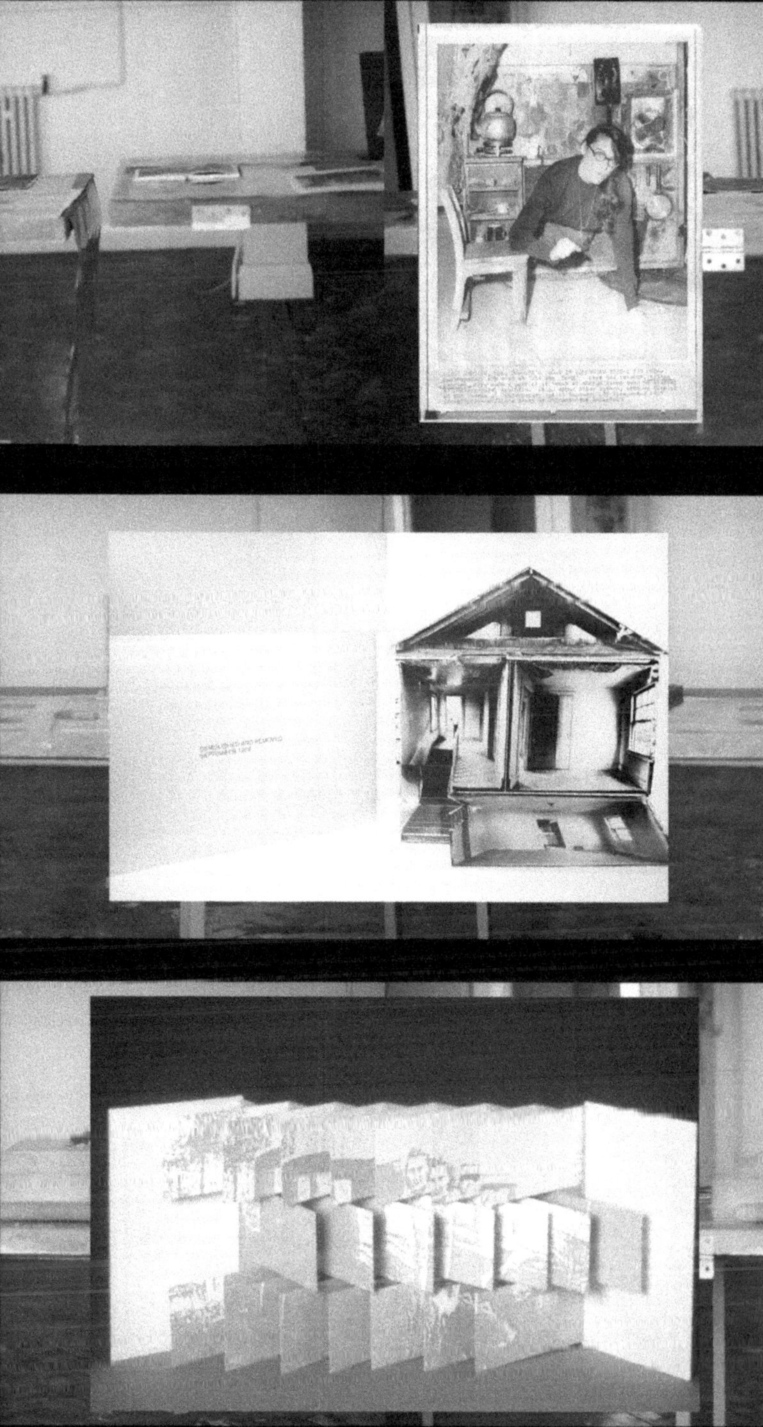

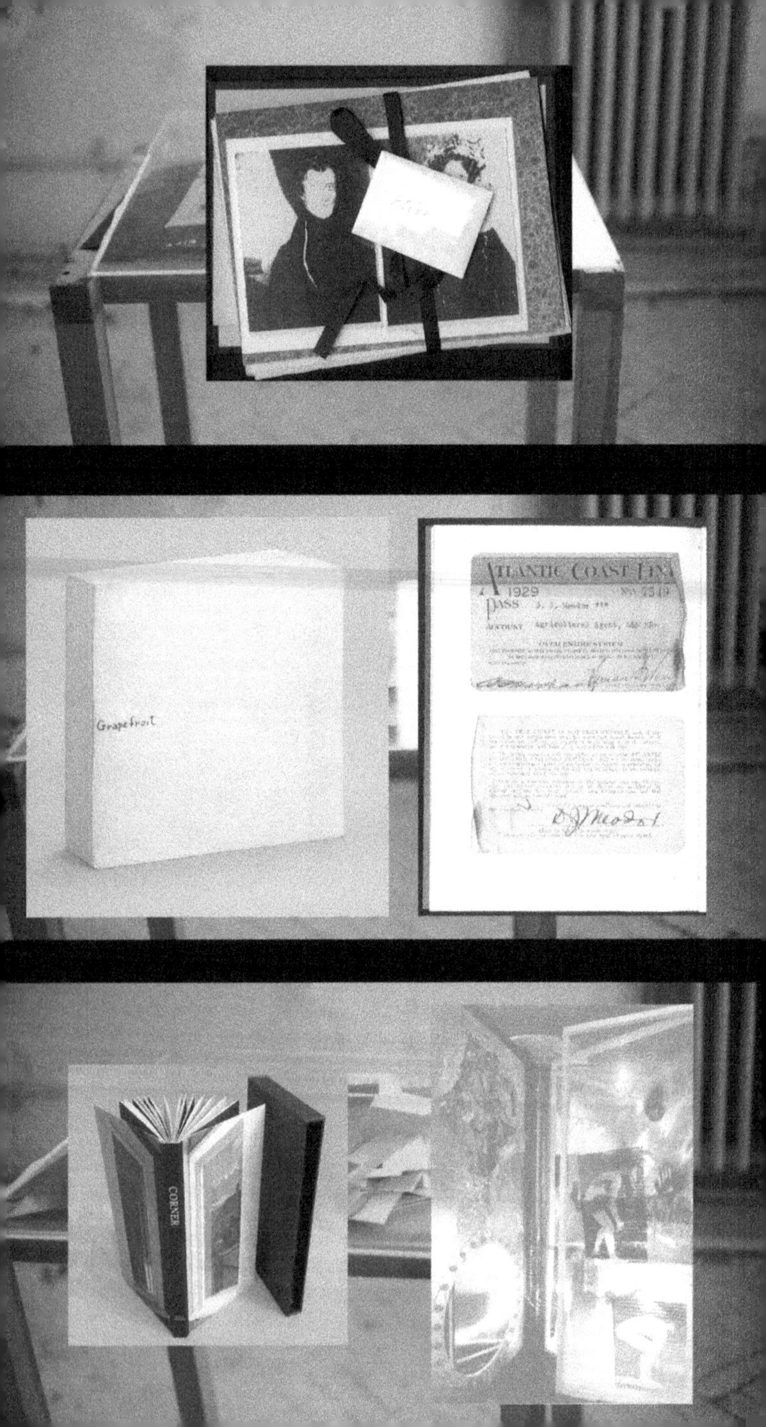

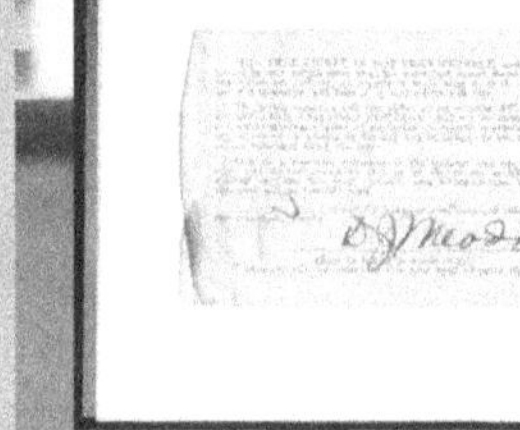
ATLANTIC COAST LINE
1929
PASS
OVER ENTIRE SYSTEM

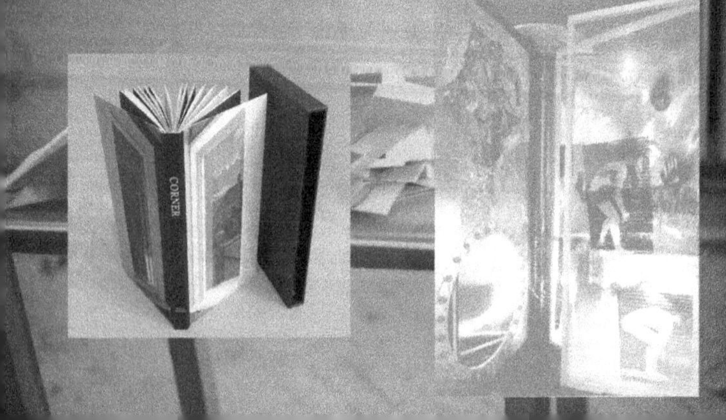
CORNER

ALL

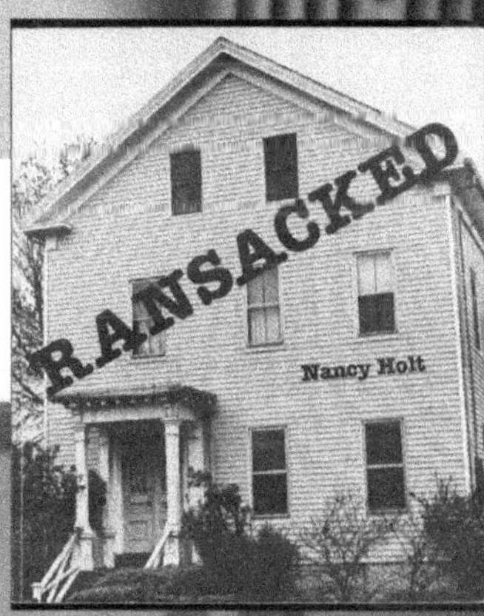

RANSACKED
Nancy Holt

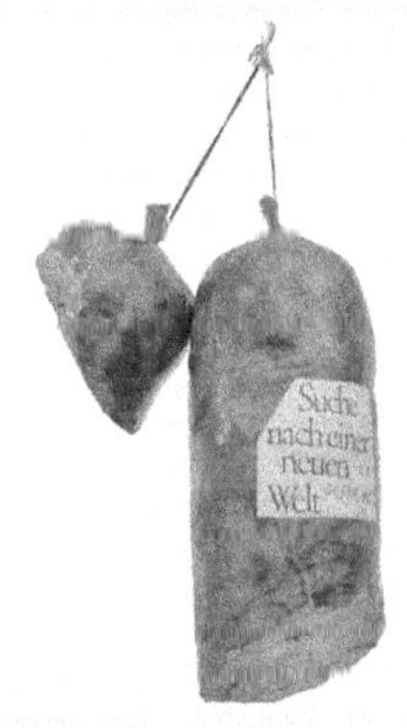

Suche nach einer neuen Welt

FOR FANS AND
SCHOLARS
* ALIKE *
ULISES CARRIÓN

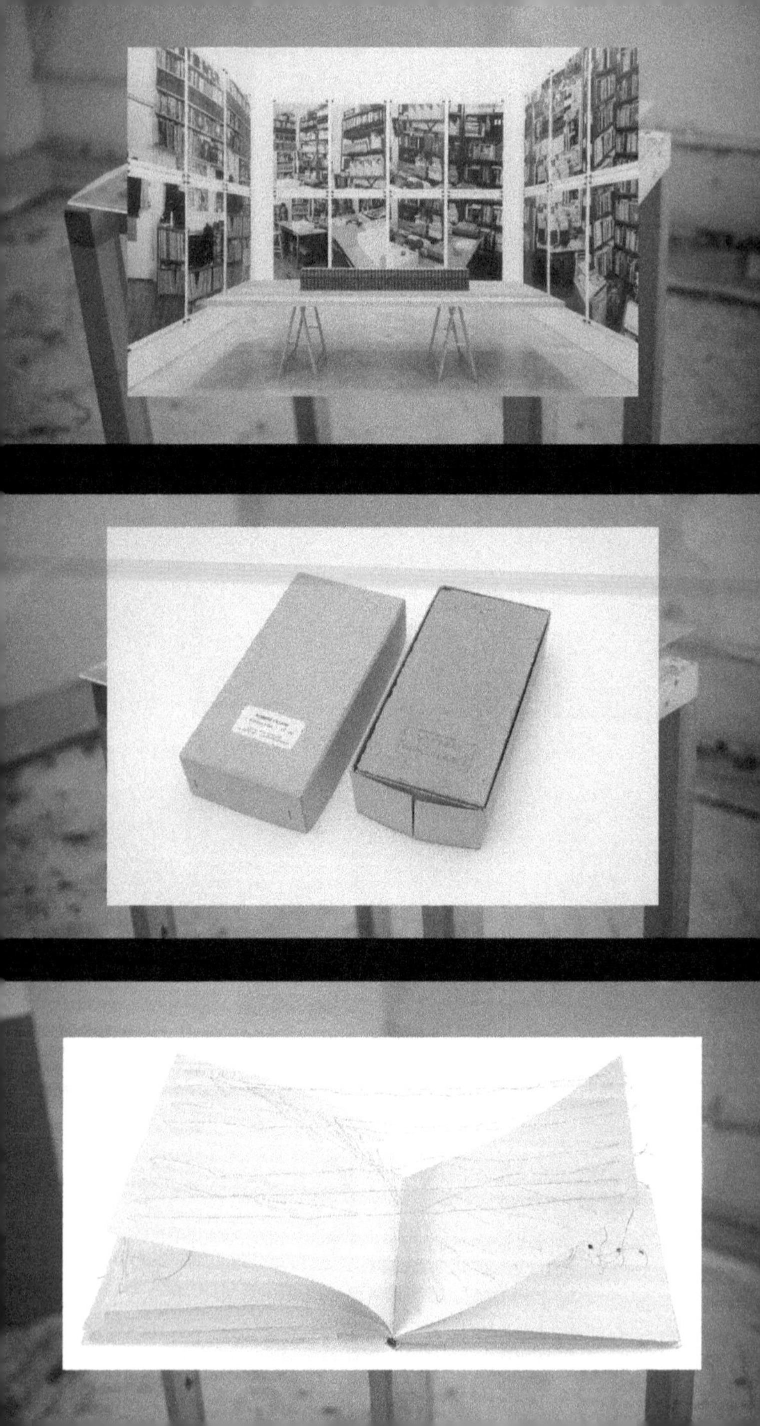

About paula roush

To begin with, we shall use paula's own comments on her approach to clarify her live / work process:

The visual interpretation of space production, from everyday spatial practice to contested spatiality, has been a consistent pursuit of my practice. Over the last five years, the focus has been the artist's house—studio—gallery, a space defined by its triple purpose of living, creating and curating.

Since 2015, I have occupied four different live—work self-contained units, all interim spaces located in South—East

London. I transformed them into temporary house–studio–galleries and my photographic practice became an enquiry focused on its intimate spaces and outdoors context, an expanded container for domestic life, artistic production and exhibition–making.

These interim spaces, being first and foremost archaeological sites of the contemporary past, provide opportunities to explore a variety of methodologies for photographic practice, including psychogeography and autoethnography.

How to represent the psychic experience of architecture and urban space? Trace the buildings' past histories, the personal and social narratives contained within their walls, memories of industrial labour, materials and services? How to document my presence and involvement in the transition into cultural economies?

My research project into photobook publishing has developed in parallel, each bookwork mirroring this probing into the psychic nature of architecture and the poetics of lived space, both interiors and urbanscape.

The reading experience is, in each case, an interplay between the architecture of the building and the visual structure of the book.[5]

paula introduces herself as photographer and founder of msdm,[6] a house—studio—gallery for photographic practice. In her works she interweaves her own photography with orphan photographs, found objects and media—archival research to draw links between experiences of contemplative photography and synchronicity in everyday life. The presentation formats include: installation, art publishing,

5 See paula roush, "house—studio—gallery." msdm.org.uk/house-studio-gallery/ (accessed January 8, 2020).

6 msdm is the acronym for mobile strategies of display & mediation, see msdm.org.uk/about (accessed January 8, 2020).

performative installation and curatorial projects.

She is a lecturer in art photography and photobook publishing in the School of Arts and Creative Industries at the London South Bank University. Her photobooks include *Nothing to Undo, Bus-Spotting+A Story, Super-Private* and *Queer Paper Gardens.* They are in public collections, including Victoria & Albert Museum's National Art Library, London and Metropolitan Museum of Art (MET), New York. They've also been recognised by Kassel and Arles Photobook Awards and Sheffield International Artists' Books Award.[7]

7 Ibid

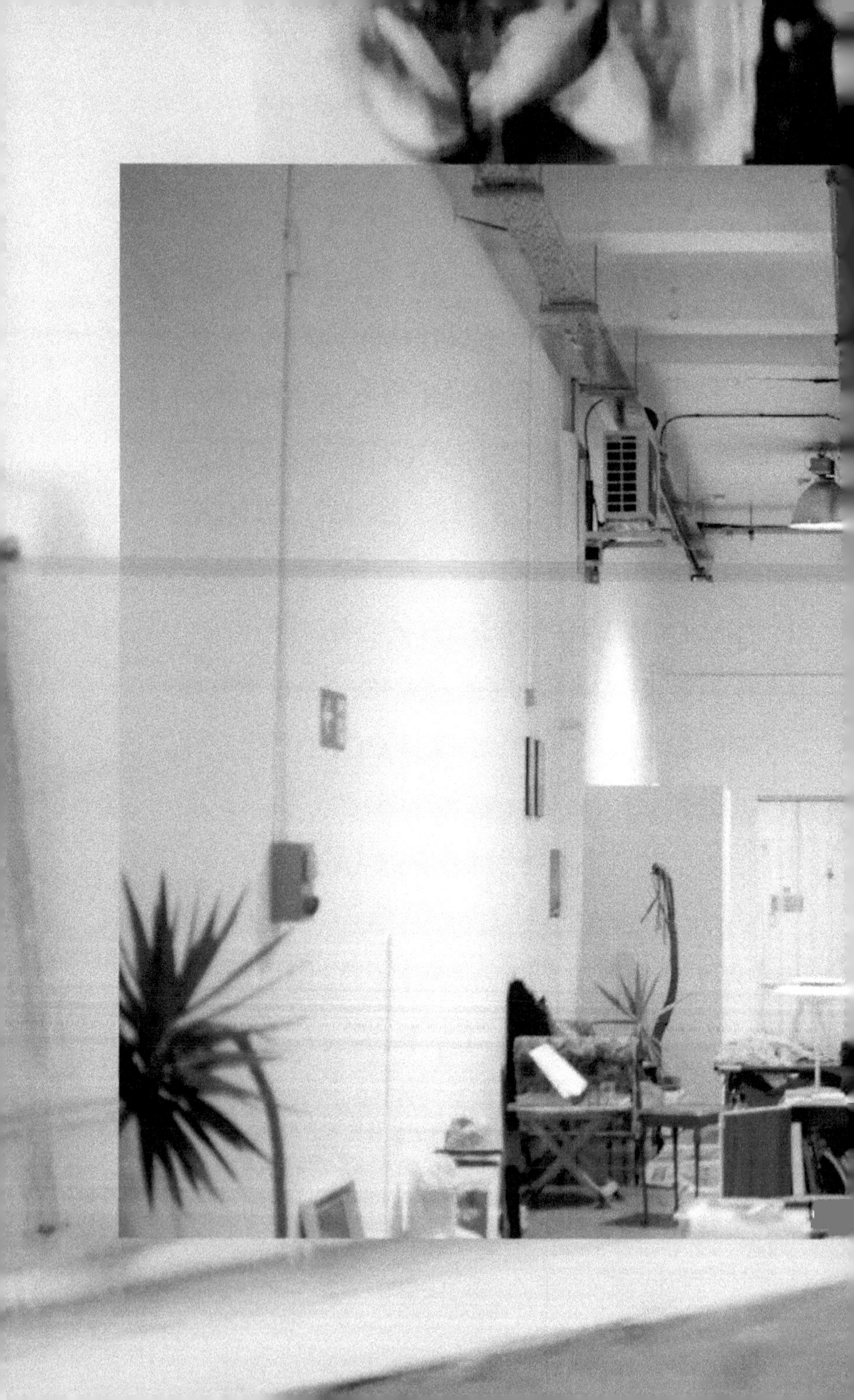

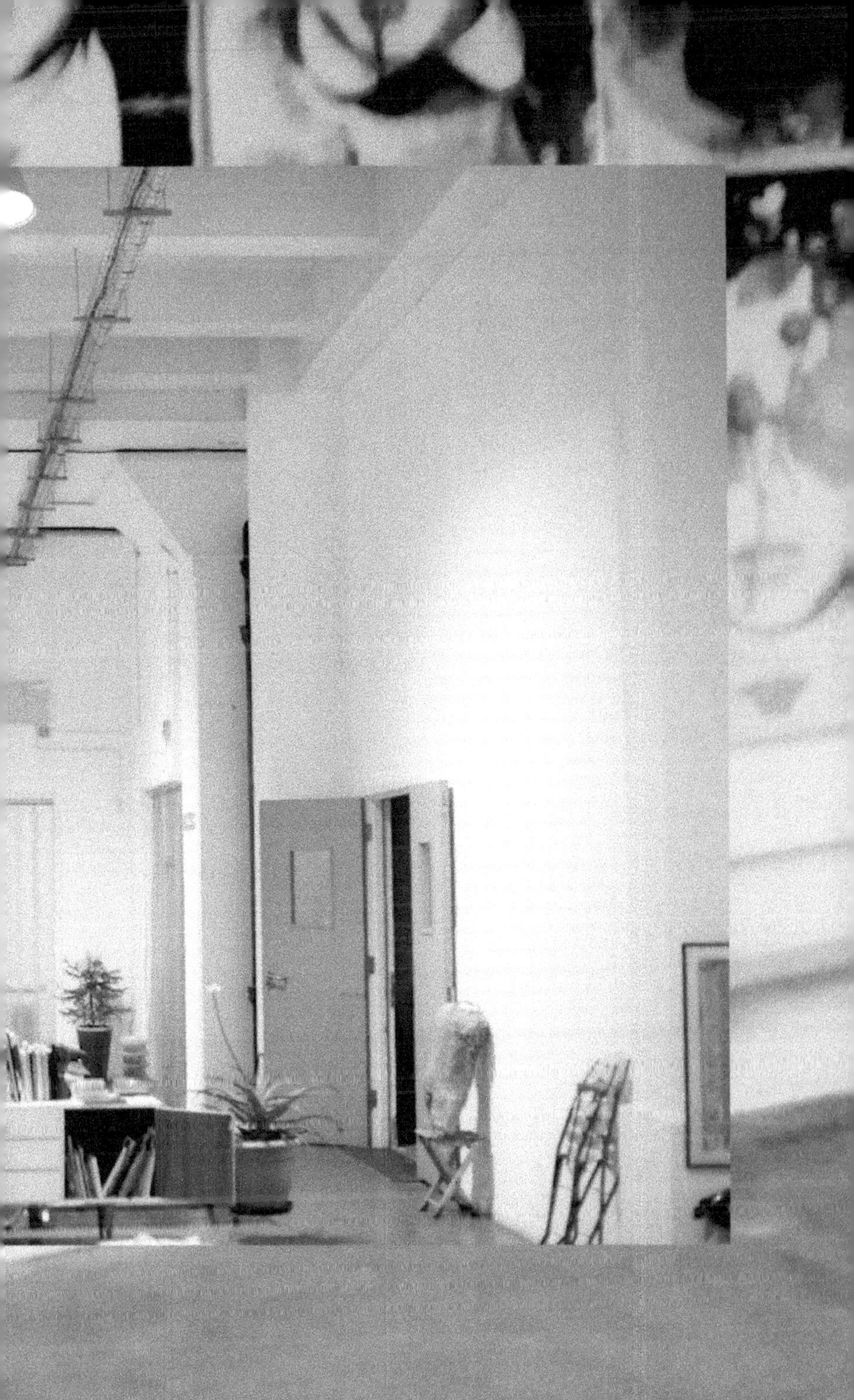

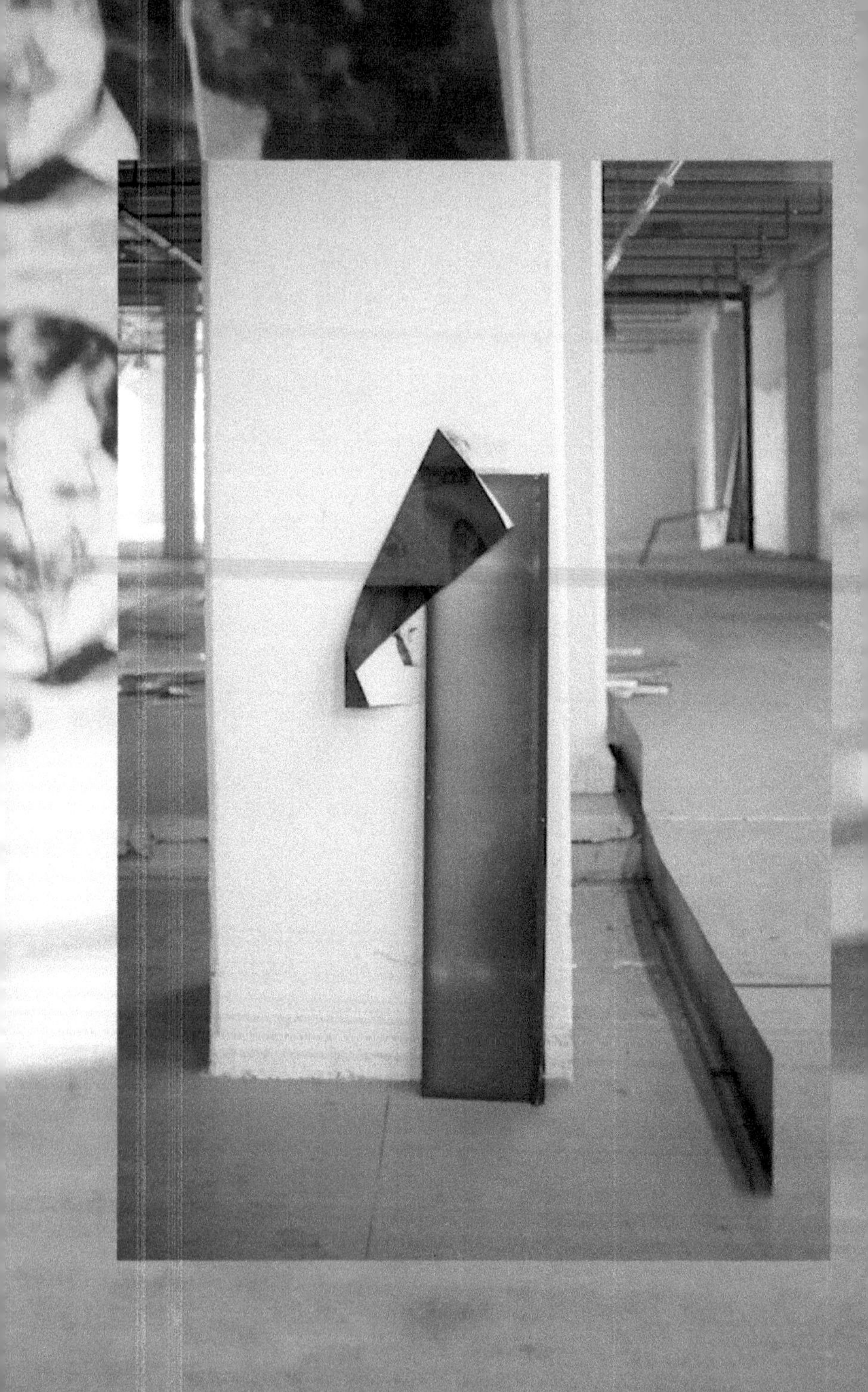

To be a property caretaker

The possibility of occupying large buildings is fundamental for the realisation of paula's life and work. These are interim spaces available for a limited period of time, and for a hybrid use that combines live–work spaces with exhibition spaces. Their spatial typologies are interchangeable and due to their scale, even after adding furniture and artwork, they appear empty. This results in the spatial juxtaposition — in a state of permanent mutability — of artefacts related to a triple interconnected experience of:

location, a recombinant structure
of new juxtapositions, lending
itself into new 'final' objects.
This process reflects the
permanent reformulation of
her personal identity that takes
place through the constant and
inseparable flow of life and work.

This *modus operandi* is only
possible due to paula's condition
of property caretaker, that
is, her ability to occupy real
estate properties that are in a
transitional period when they are
no longer in use and awaiting their
reintegration into the real estate
market or possible architectural
intervention.

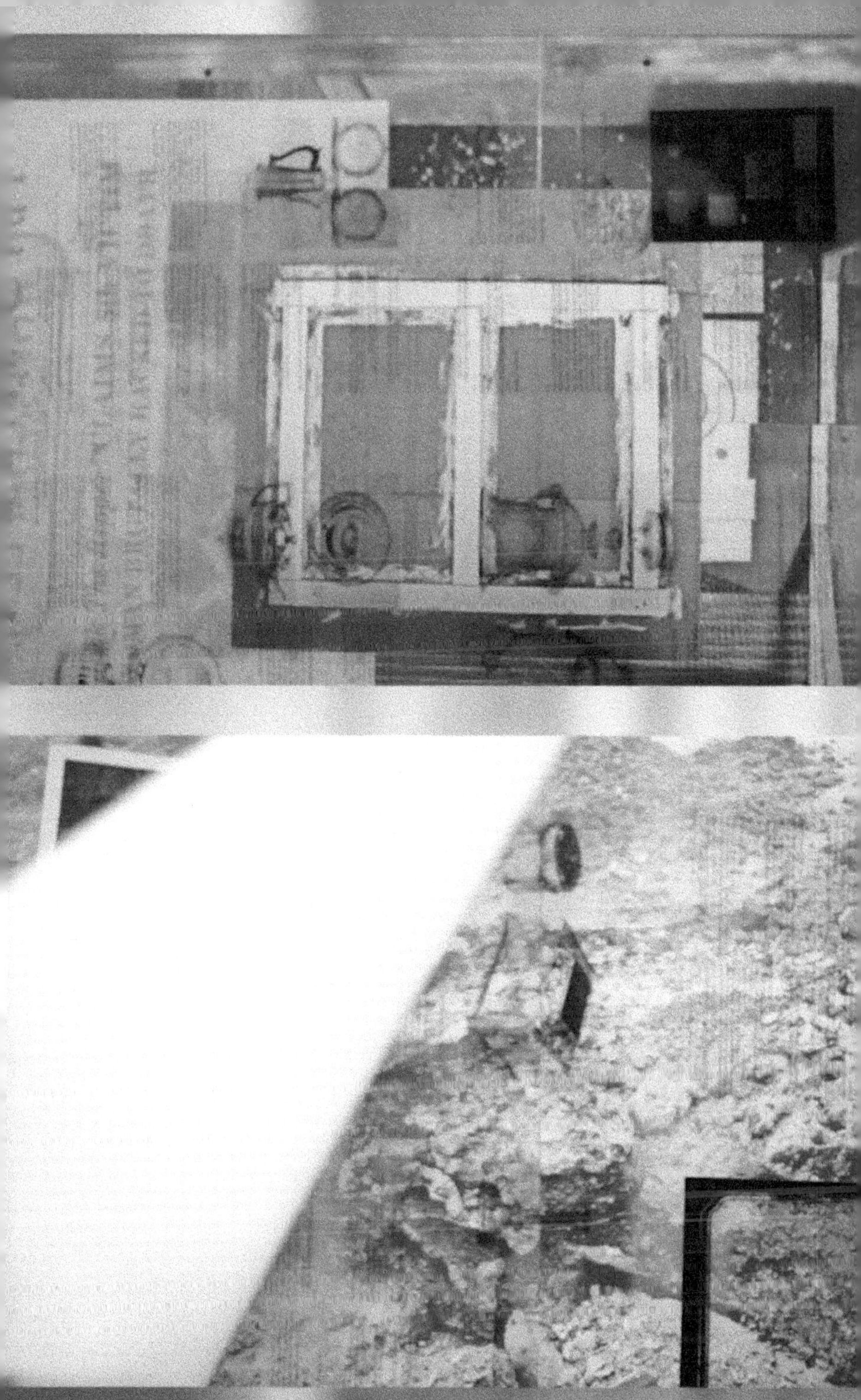

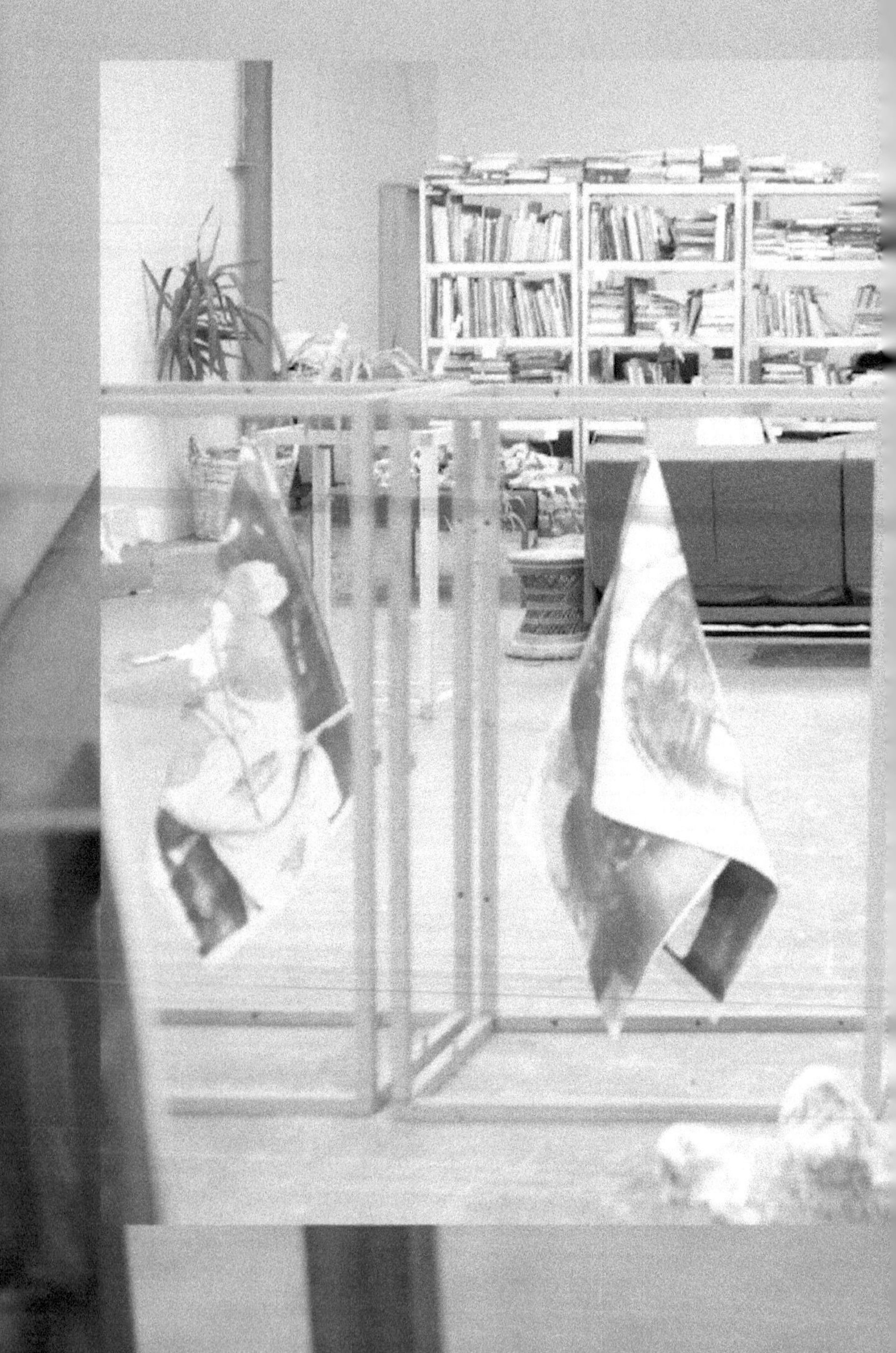

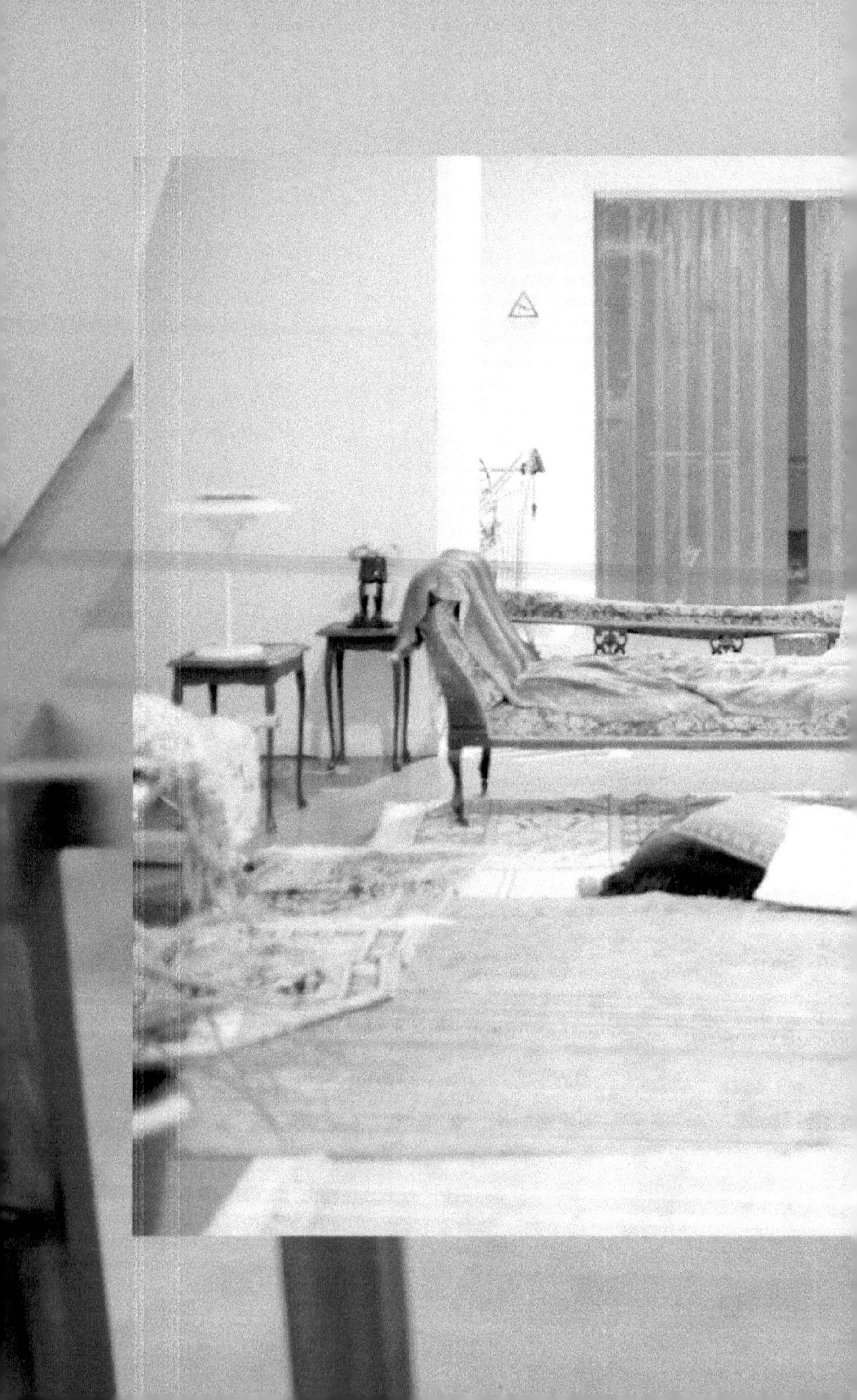

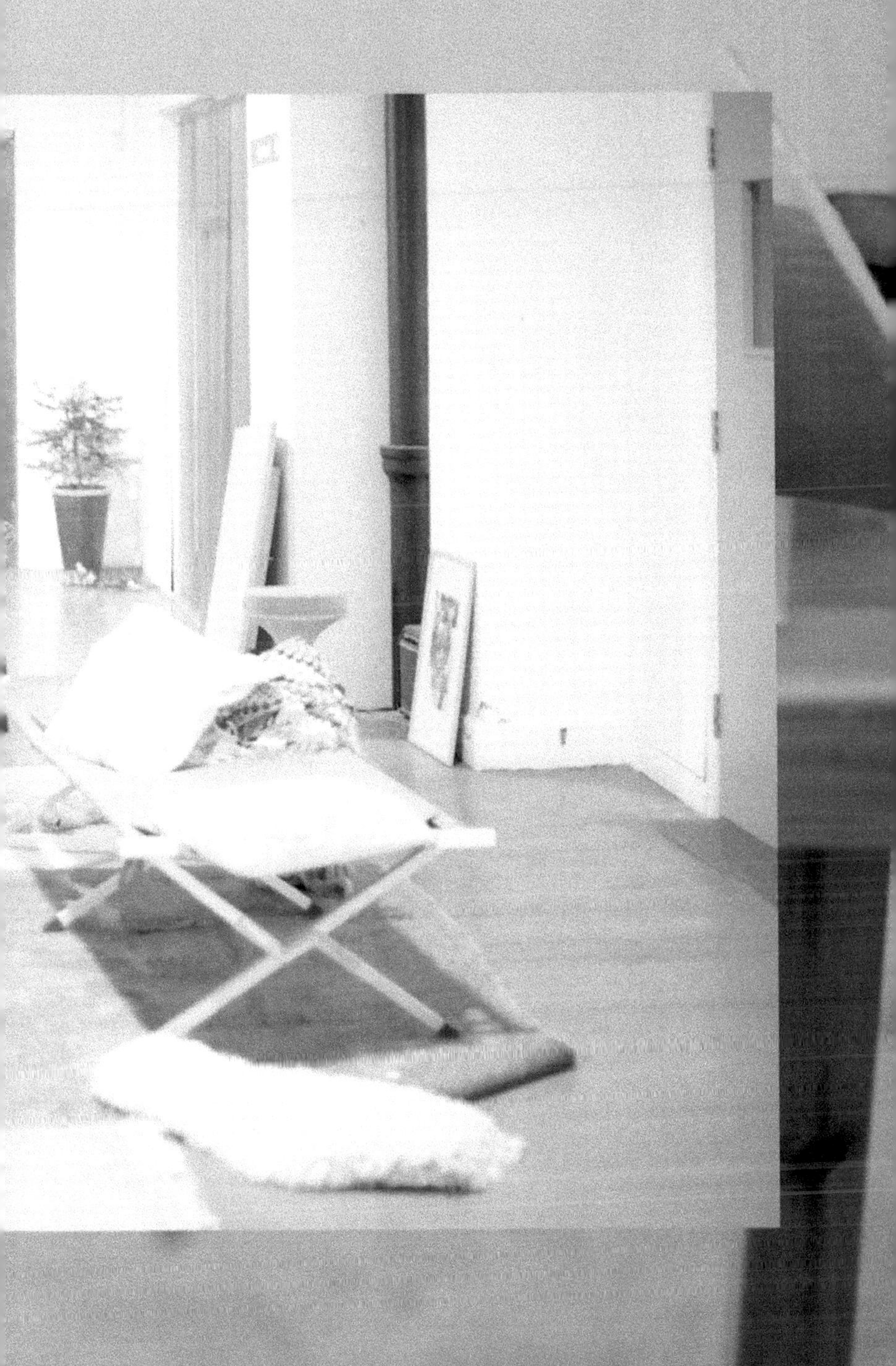

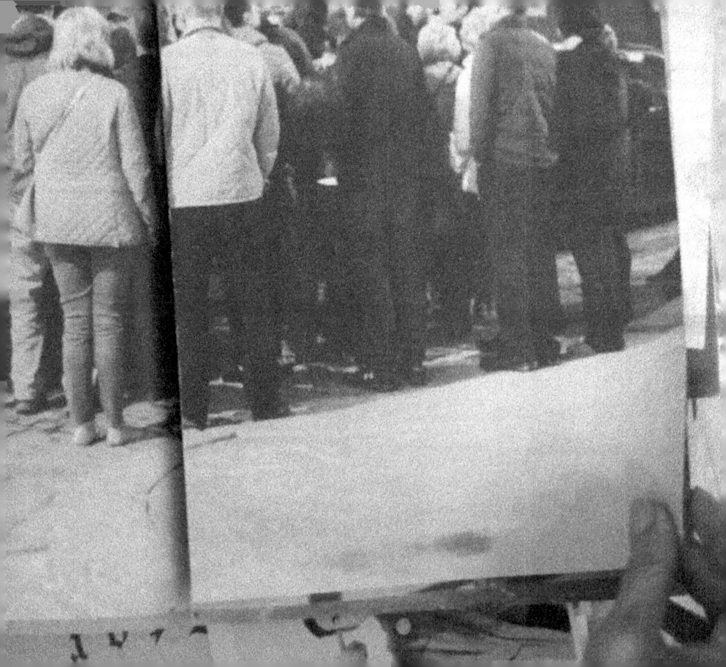

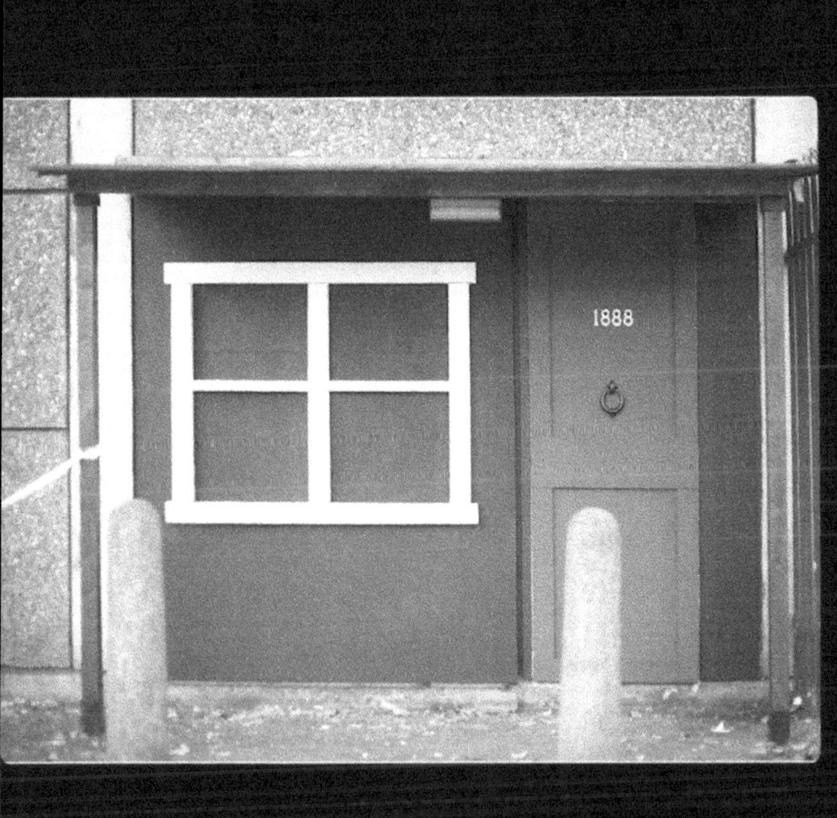

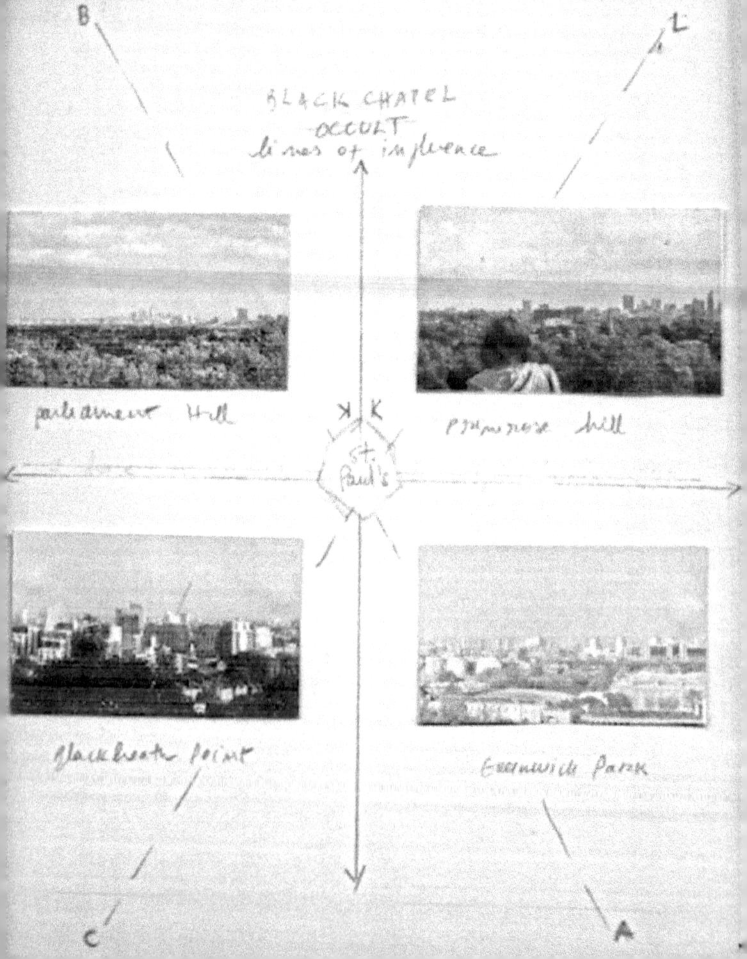

B

A

BLACK CHAPEL
OCCULT
lines of influence

parliament hill

primrose hill

K K

St. Paul's

Blackheath Point

Greenwich Park

C

A

The expanded field of contemporaneity

In order to define what we mean by an expanded practice and, by analogy, what an expanded book can be, I use the reflection that Delfim Sardo articulates around Rosalind Krauss's concept of sculpture in the expanded field:

...sculpture in the 20th century consists of a permanent reworking of the absence of a body that is no longer there — because it is elsewhere, because it has been metamorphosed, because there is only a hint left of it. In that process, sculpture

is expanded; it is expanded so much that it ceases to be itself to become the most difficult artistic genre to define, the most difficult to circumscribe...[8]

We can extrapolate this condition of the metamorphosed object to the artist's book: only a hint left behind, replacing a body that is no longer there.

Let's take the example of <u>Blackchapel</u> project.
It is a book that incorporates and works through paula's personal feelings in relation to the space she occupied in Whitechapel from 2015 to 2017. It is a psychogeographic investigation

8 Delfim Sardo, "O Enorme Campo Do Que Não Tem Nome," in *O Exercício Experimental da Liberdade* (Lisboa: Orfeu Negro, 2017), 140.

of East London, with literary references to the occult mythology of Whitechapel including photographic evidence related to Jack the Ripper's Whitechapel crimes. And it is also, in my opinion, a projection of her own anxieties regarding the immense deserted space of the building she occupied.

Psychogeographic research is complemented with further documentation connected with the planning application for the site and related panoramic vistas of London, sourced from architectural codes of practice.

This bookwork is not officially published yet and is still undergoing a reformulation, where different narrative voices are tried out. There is an edition narrated from a personal point of view, in which paula puts herself in the role of the photographer, tracing her experience, including moving into the building and discovering the occult sources; and there is another edition told from an investigative perspective, unfolding in a third person, where her role is that of an editor that organises and sequences the material 'reaching her hands.'

All the materials mobilised in this project—her own photographs, artefacts sourced from the building site, literary research and archival material—were used in the exhibition *Evidencing The East End,* first installed in the Stepney

Way warehouse, Whitechapel,
in 2017,[9] inaugurating the spatial
model of the house–studio–
gallery. This material has been
reconfigured in the current
space in Woolwich, being
distributed in several 'clusters'
or 'constellations,' together
with other elements of different
provenance, some in the state of
'sandwiches.'

I can see in this constant
reworking and multiple
reconfiguring of materials the
metamorphosis that Delfim Sardo
identifies in the field of expanded
sculpture, made visible in the
ongoing corporeal mutation of

9 *Evidencing The East End: paula roush Julie Cook*, two photobookworks
  photographed at 85 Stepney Way Warehouse, Whitechapel London, presented
  as a double site-specific installation, May 2017. msdm.org.uk/evidencing-east-
  end/ [Accessed January 8, 2020).

the publication, becoming an expanded practice of the book. I can also find in this work process the mutability that allows it to exist beyond a specific time frame.

The contamination that results from the aggregation of materials from different sources and contexts (which constitute the 'sandwiches of materials,' the installations, the agglomerations and the books) fits into the contemporary condition that Nuno Crespo describes as follows:

> *Creative and exhibition practices are characterised, according to Bishop, by the effort to trace the physiognomy of the present. This physiognomy is temporal*

and is characterised by an anachronistic dynamic, that is, the artistic present is a place of contamination that develops a non-chronological horizon containing the possibility of making multiple crossings, syntheses, collages and junctions.

That is why Didi-Huberman, when trying to think art history, proposes an atemporal methodology and, following Warburg, pathological looking for logics of influences and contaminations and not affiliations or chronologies.[10]

10 Nuno Crespo, "Ser pontual num encontro que só pode falhar. Notas sobre a contemporaneidade do artista." In P. Hussak (Ed.), *Poiésis, Arte contemporânea: anacronismo e pós-conceitualismo* (Florianópolis. Editora Federal Fluminense, 2016), 26-27.

We can also infer that the live–work method used by paula (which I call 'immersive') is similar to the process she uses to make books and the subsequent objects that derive from them, whether 'constellations' of materials or 'sandwiches.'

This is Crespo's 'anachronistic condition' where *"the artistic present is a place of contamination,"* and the visual structure of the work organised according to a logic that is not chronological, but follows other logics. This 'immersion' process, and the processes of book construction–deconstruction share the same method. In other words, life and work are 'constructed' in a similar way.

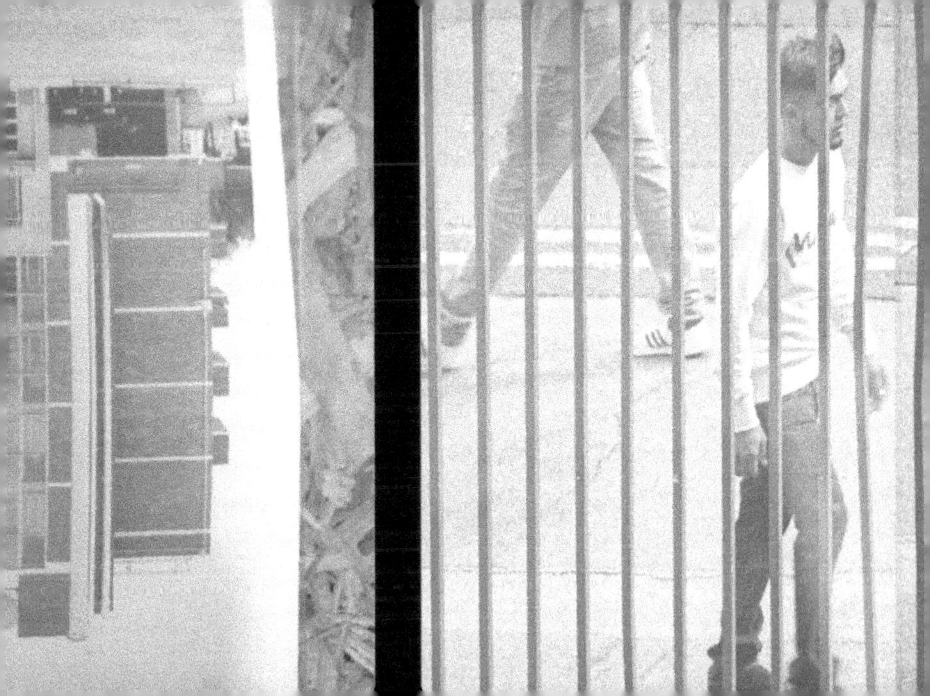

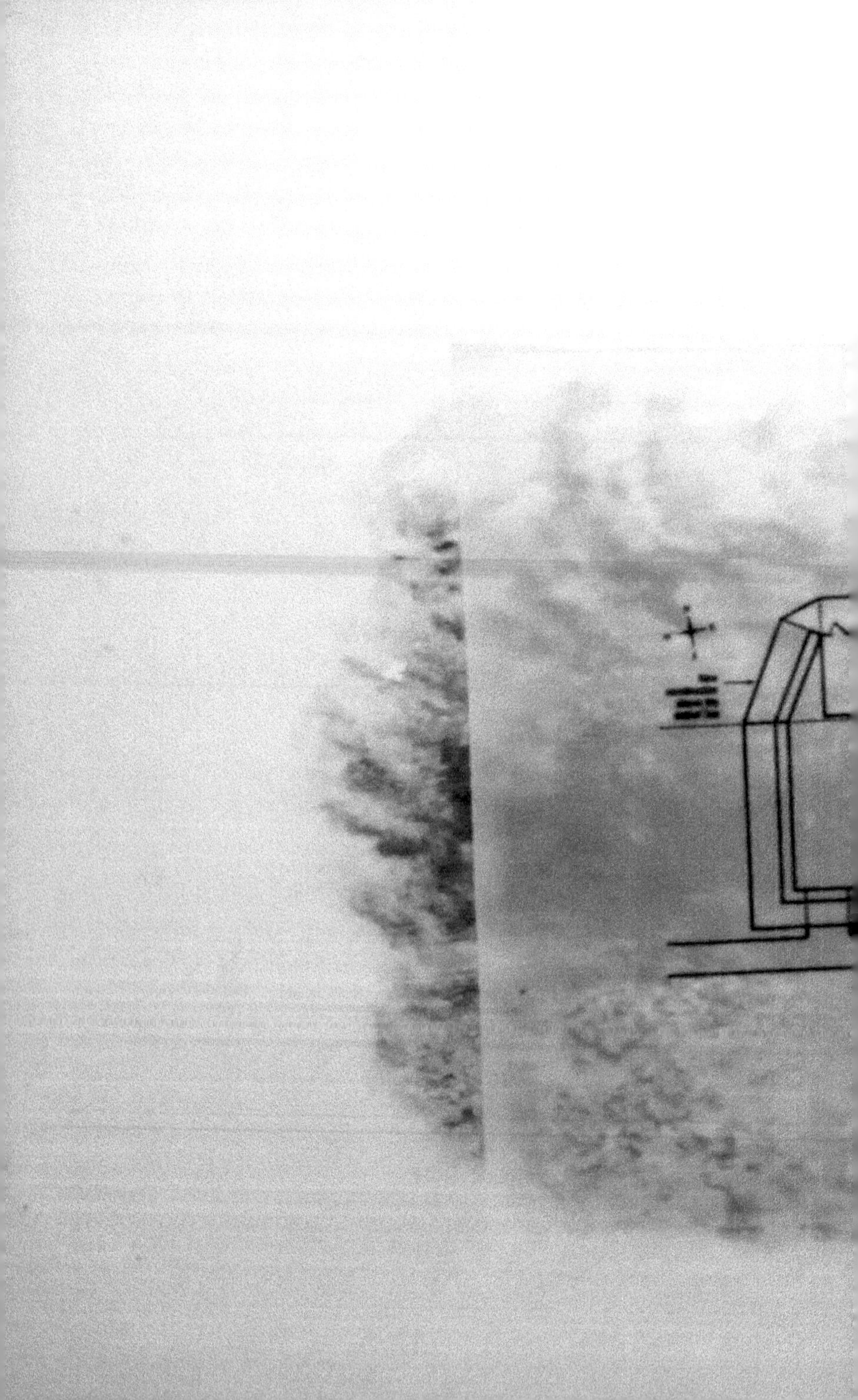

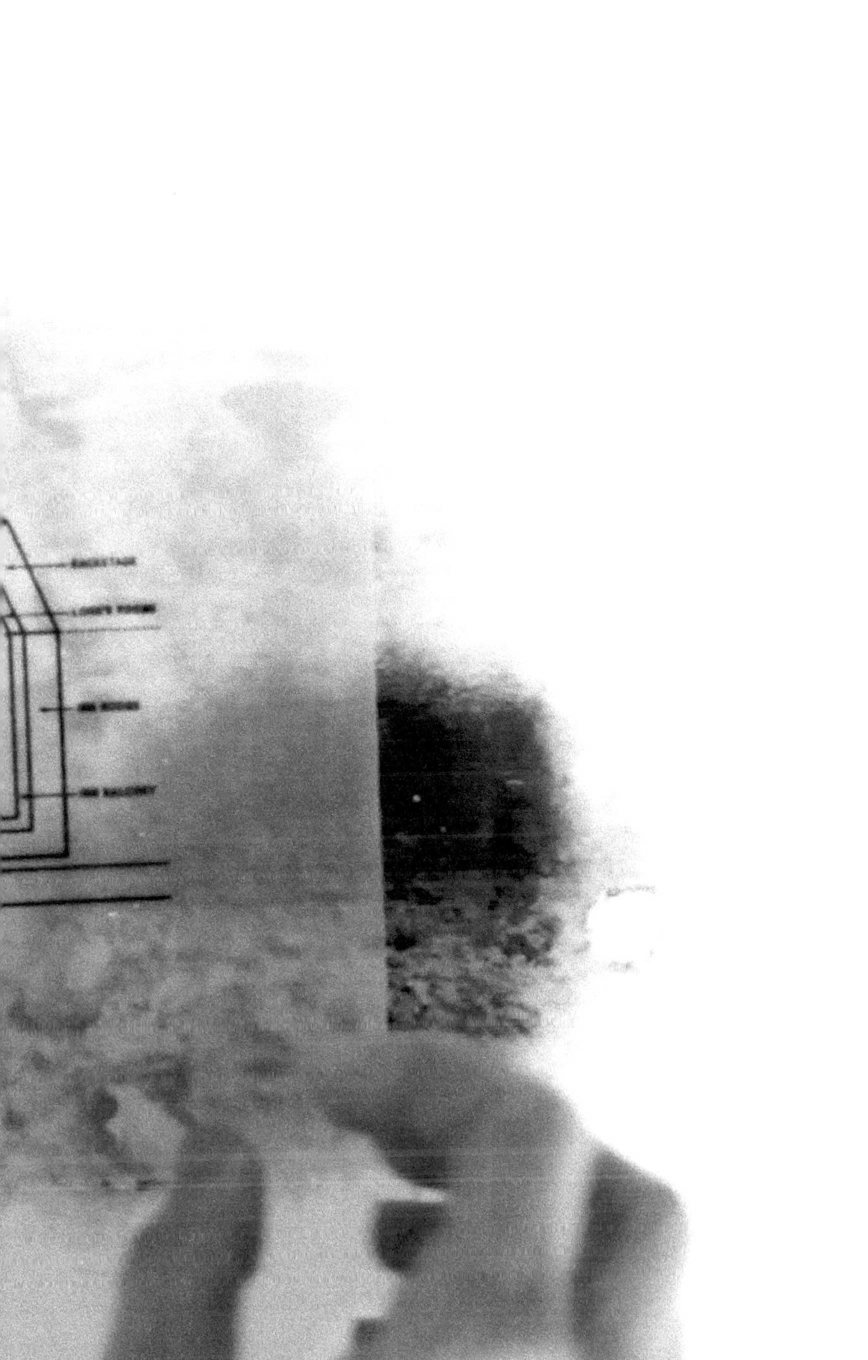

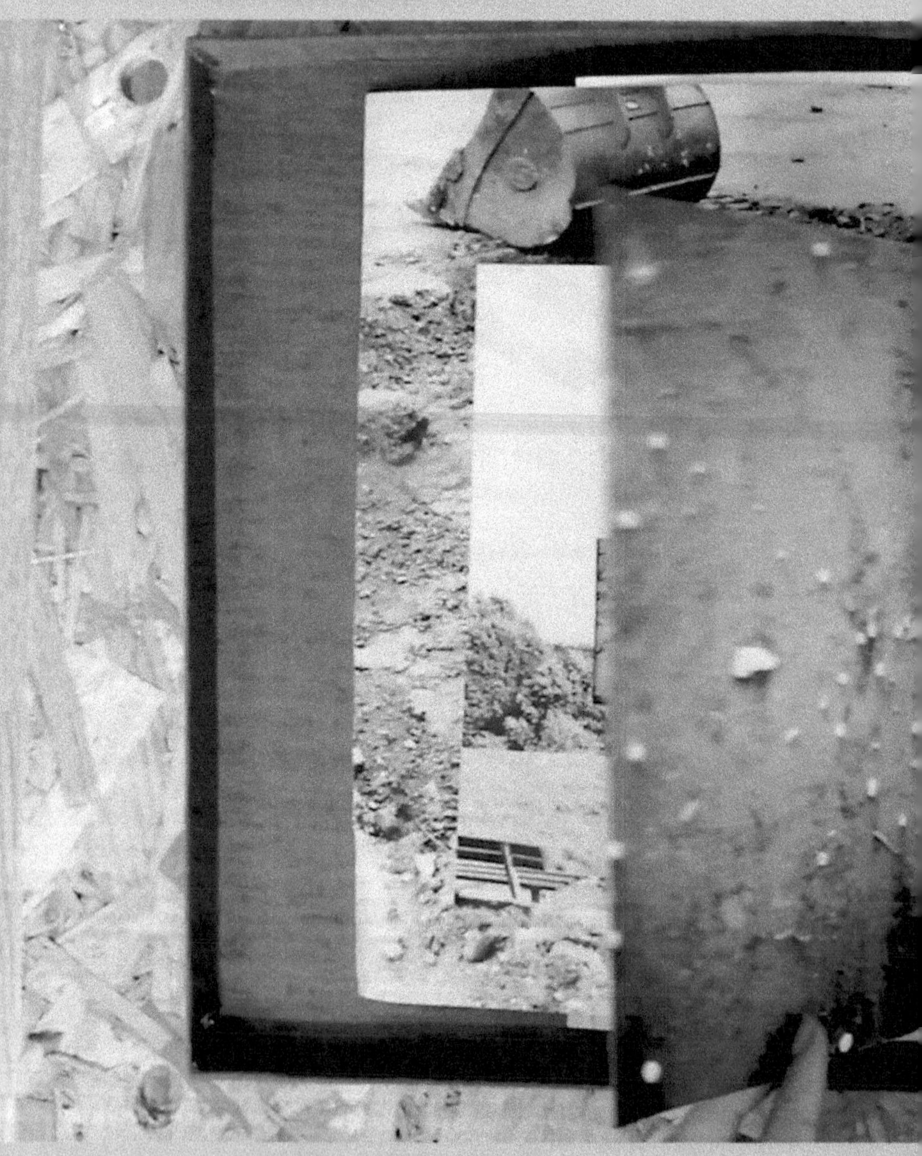

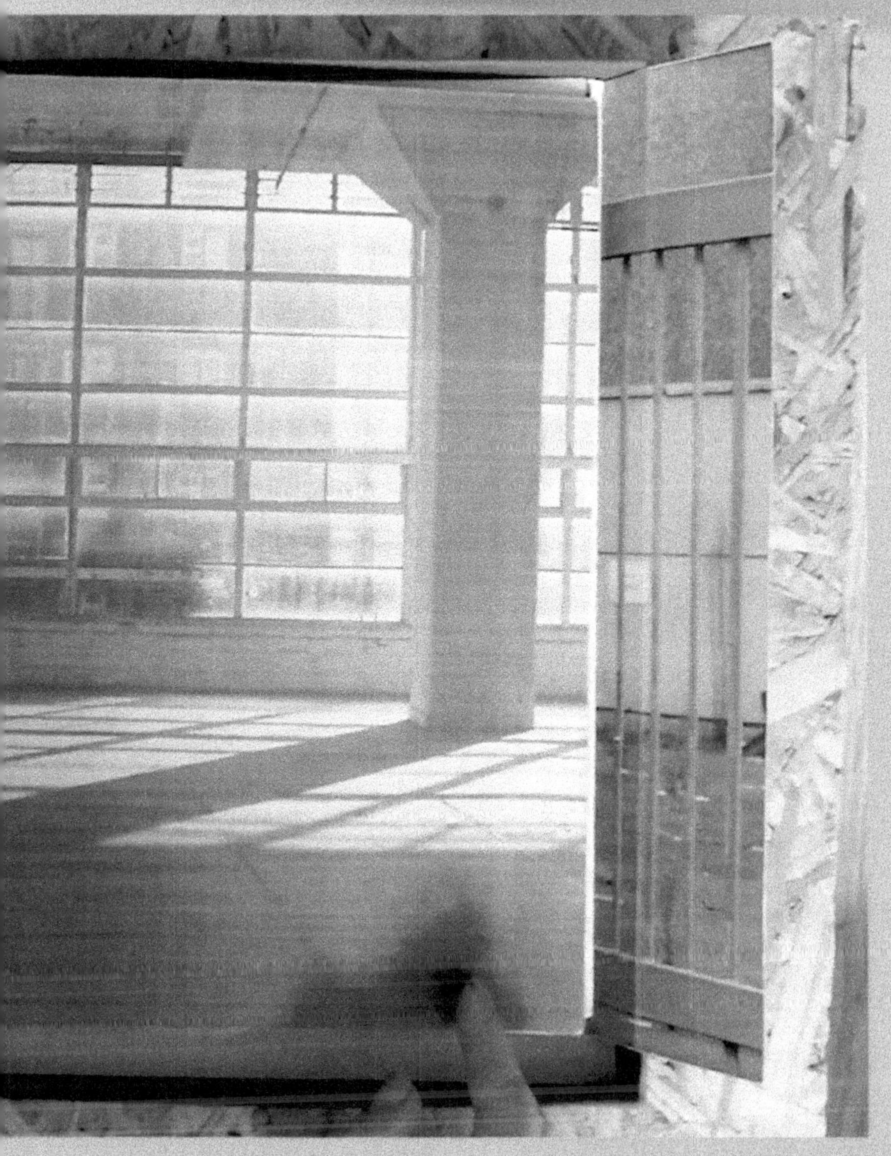

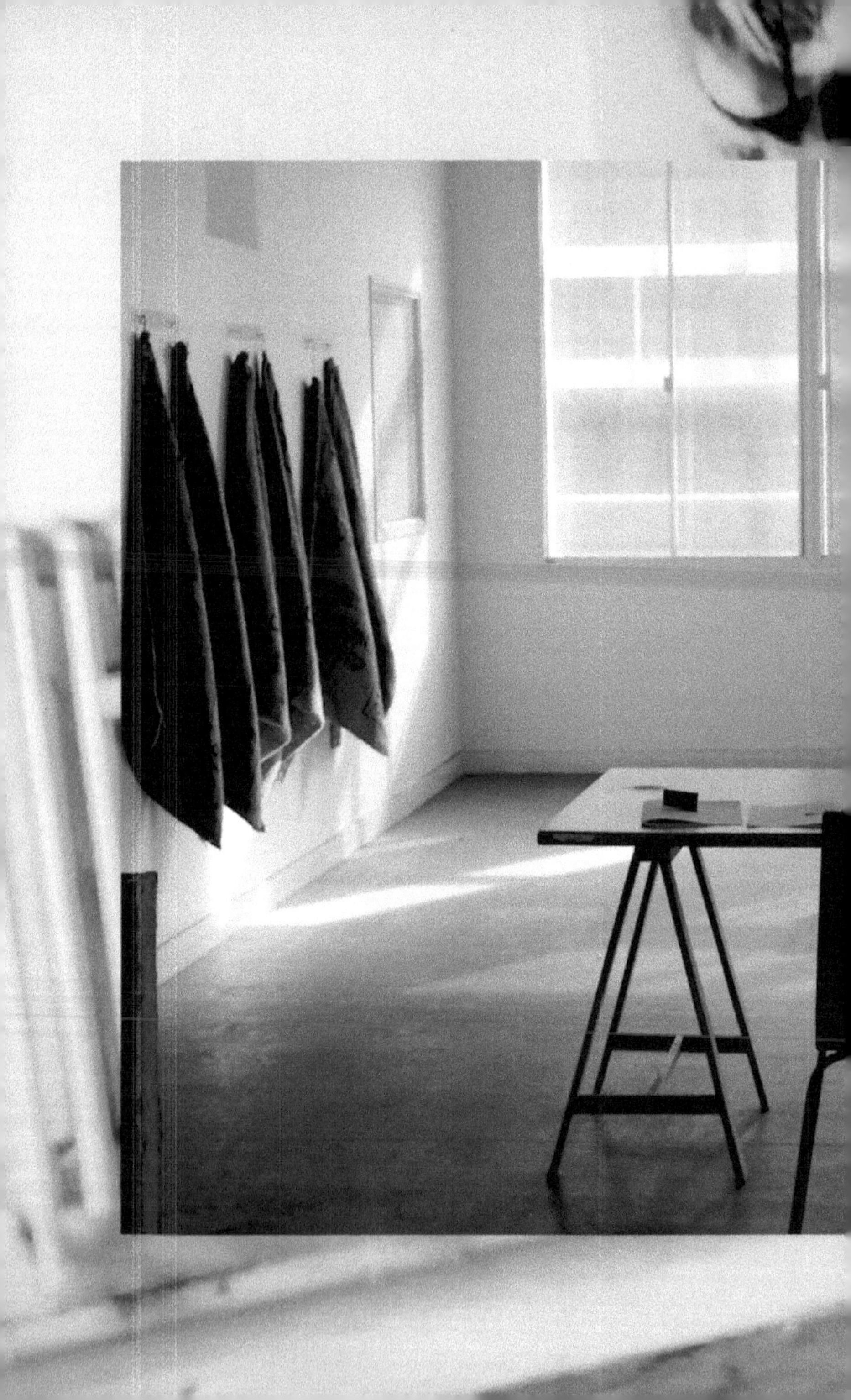

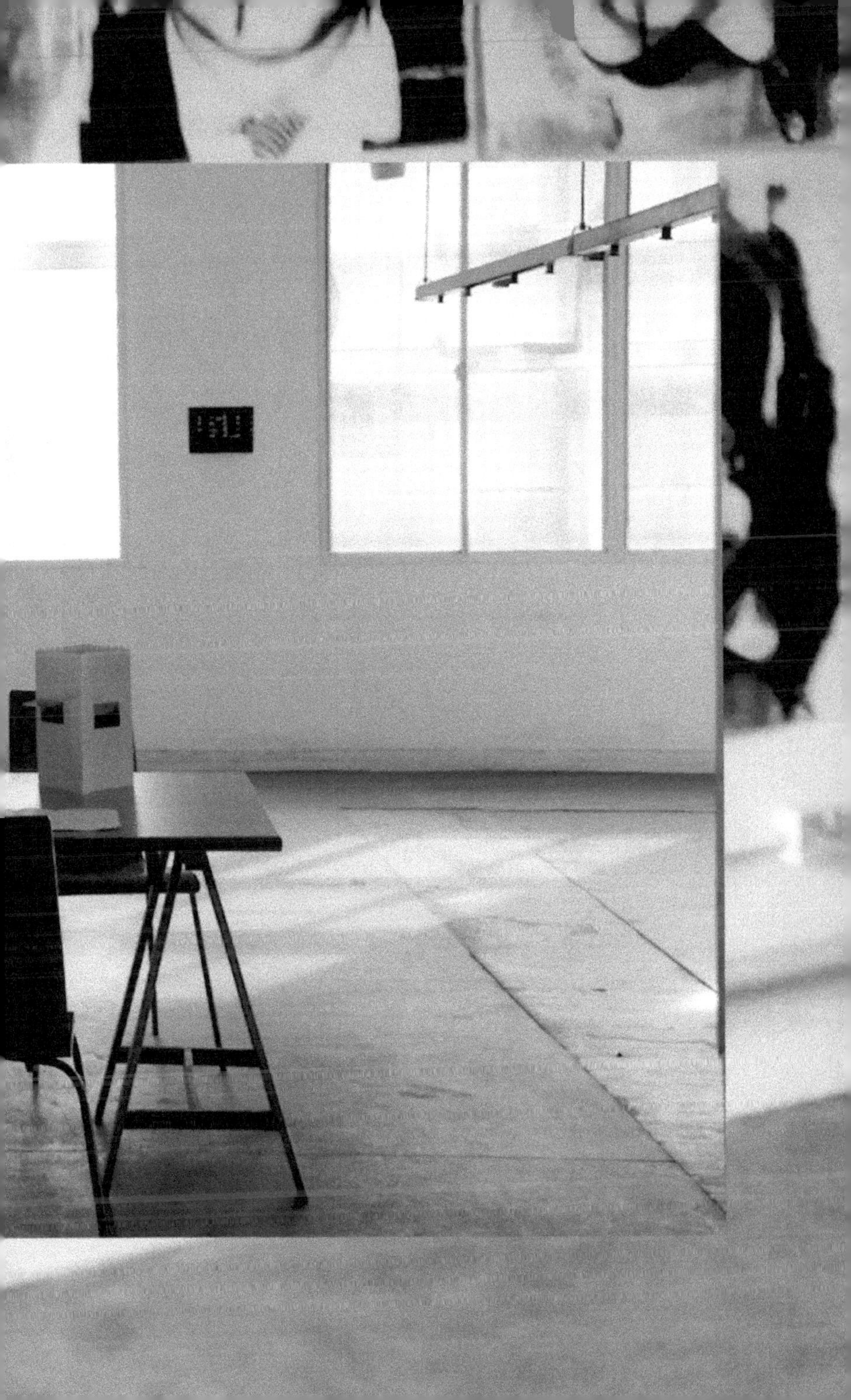

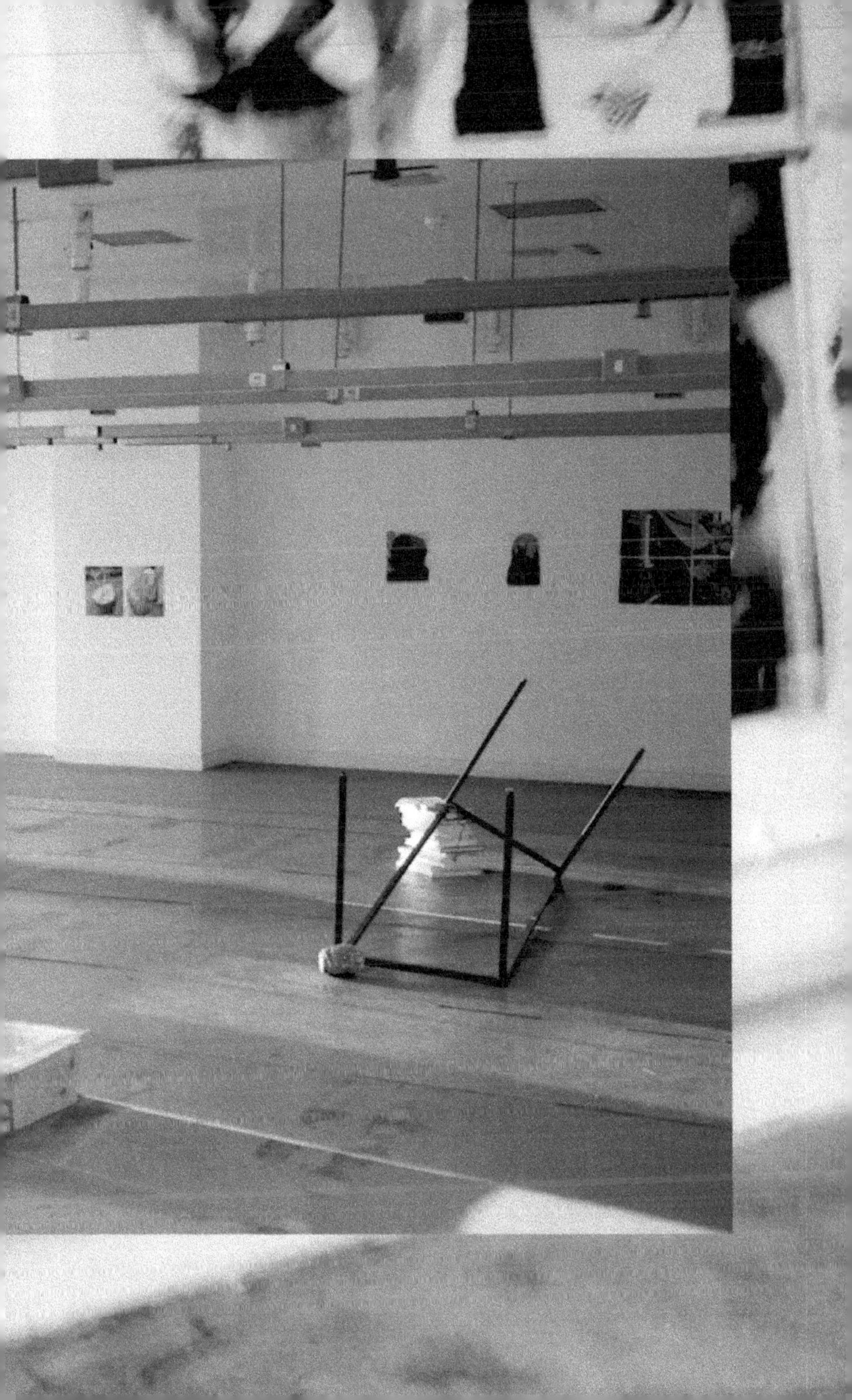

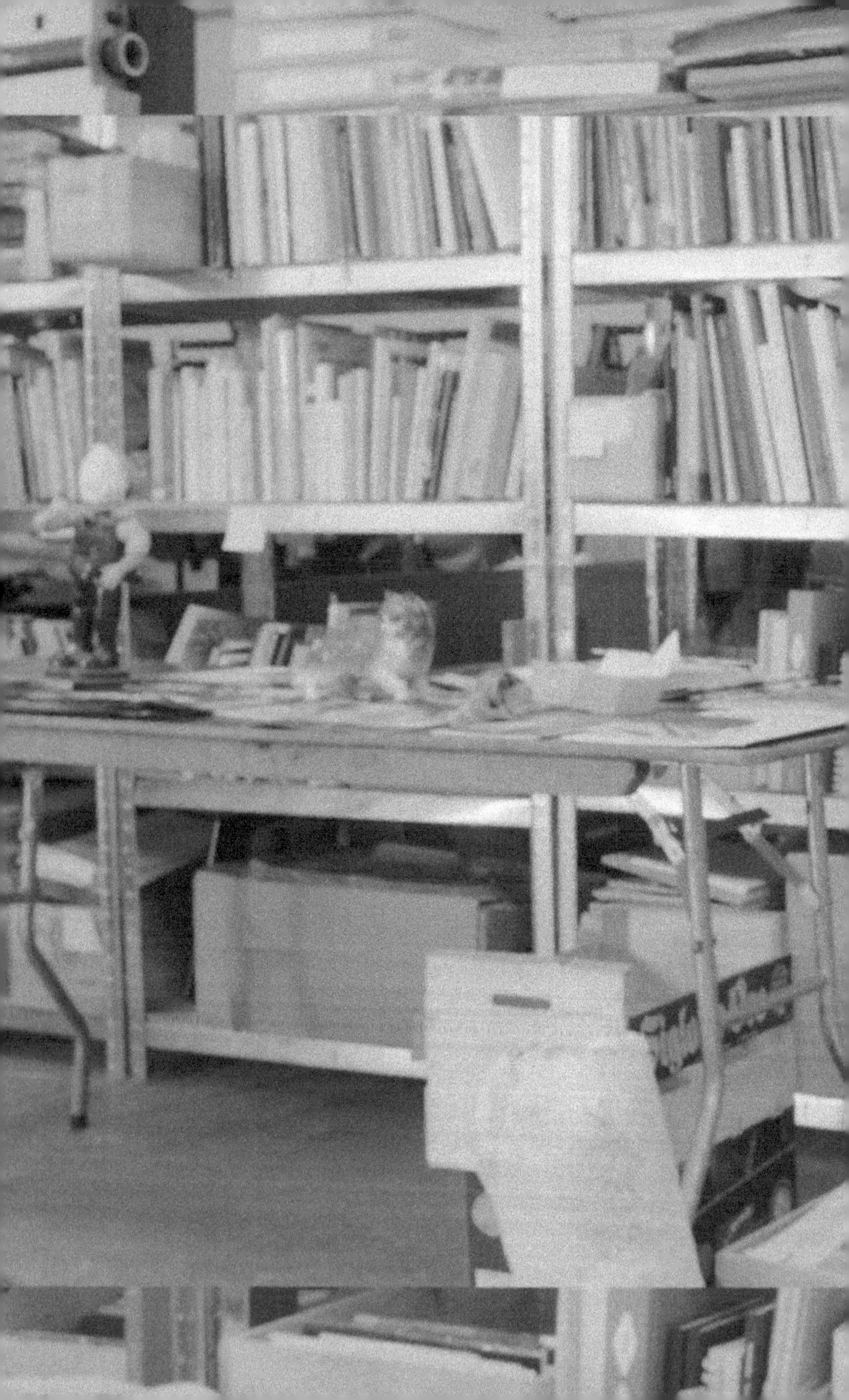

Collections and books

The issue of the similarity between collections and books is a fundamental one to clarify. Is the totality of paula's practice guided by the making of a book? We can infer this from an extract of paula's writing (in this essay) where she states that,
"The reading experience is, in each case, an interplay between the architecture of the building and the visual structure of the book."[11]

What we need to know is whether, as paula tells us, the experience of 'reading' the entire house–studio–gallery and the different 'constellations' of materials

11 see msdm.org.uk/house-studio-gallery, Ibid.

installed inside it, is similar to the reading of a book and, therefore, the occupation of the building has a visual structure similar to that of a book.

To clarify this hypothesis, we use the essay *"Books as Collections: Dieter Roth's Artists' Books as Case in Point"* by Barbara Bader,[12] identifying the 'constellations' of materials existing in the building, either as collections or as books, be they books in the strict sense, 'sandwiches' or mere agglomerations of materials.

Barbara Bader tells us in her essay that books and collections share more than an affinity in

12 Barbara Bader, "Books as Collections: Dieter Roth's Artists' Books as Case in Point," in *Journal of the Oxford University History Society*, n.3 (2005), 1-18.

their constitution. A collection is understood as a unit of objects agglomerated systematically and kept in a particular space, whether a box, an office, a room or even an entire building (note taken). She adds that a book consists of a number of pages aggregated within a cover, which together form a conceptual unit.

It appears that there is not a total identification between collection and book. However, as Bader points out, by cognitively isolating or objectifying information from the outside world, both books and collections have the ability to contextualise their content. On the notion of 'another space' or 'heterotopia,' Bader, quoting Foucault, describes them as

"places...outside of all places,"
and concurs with Kate Linker
that artists' books provide
"an alternative space."[13]

We can find in paula's 'sandwiches
of materials' that most elements
come from a photographic
matrix, albeit with different
materialities and typologies,
including typographic stencils,
photographic posters or prints
of images from publications and
even paula's own photographs
printed in large format.
Those works share the condition
referred to by Barbara Bader,
of being "another space" that
objectifies information and that

13 Michel Foucault, "Des espace autres," *Architecture/Movement/Continuite, no. 5* (1984 (original paper presented in 1967, authorised for publication fourteen years later), and Kate Linker, "The Artists' Book as an Alternative Space," *Studio International 195*, no. 990 (1980), pp 75-79.

contains, in all its elements,
a common characteristic: its
photographic provenance.

But the definitive combination of
these two 'states'—collections and
books— that includes materials as
works in progress and materials
as works of art being exhibited, is
clarified with Bader's invocation
of Ulises Carrión's essay *The New
Art of Making Books,* where the
commonality between books
and collections is attributed to
their temporal or spatiotemporal
dimension.

By defining the pages of a book
as *"a sequence of spaces"* he calls
attention to the fact that the act of
reading and of turning the pages
demands time and, consequently,

that the book must be perceived as a "space–time sequence."

As we know from experience, moving through time and space — literally or metaphorically — is fundamental to any collection, be it in a gallery or museum, or the more intimate context of a collection of stamps or coins. Both the curator and the book designer have a wide range of strategies to slow down or speed up the narrative, and consequently to influence the beholder's movements and spatiotemporal experiences.[14]

In other words, the 'sandwiches of materials,' be they installations,

14 Ulises Carrion, *The New Art of Making Books*, in *Quant aux livres/On Books*, ed. Juan J. Agius (Geneva: Héros-Limite, 1997), p. 129.

agglomerations or books, when inserted in the space of the house–studio–gallery, all share this condition of being part of a space–time sequence and share with the building a narrative structure.
And this, we conclude, provides an experience similar to the reading of a book.

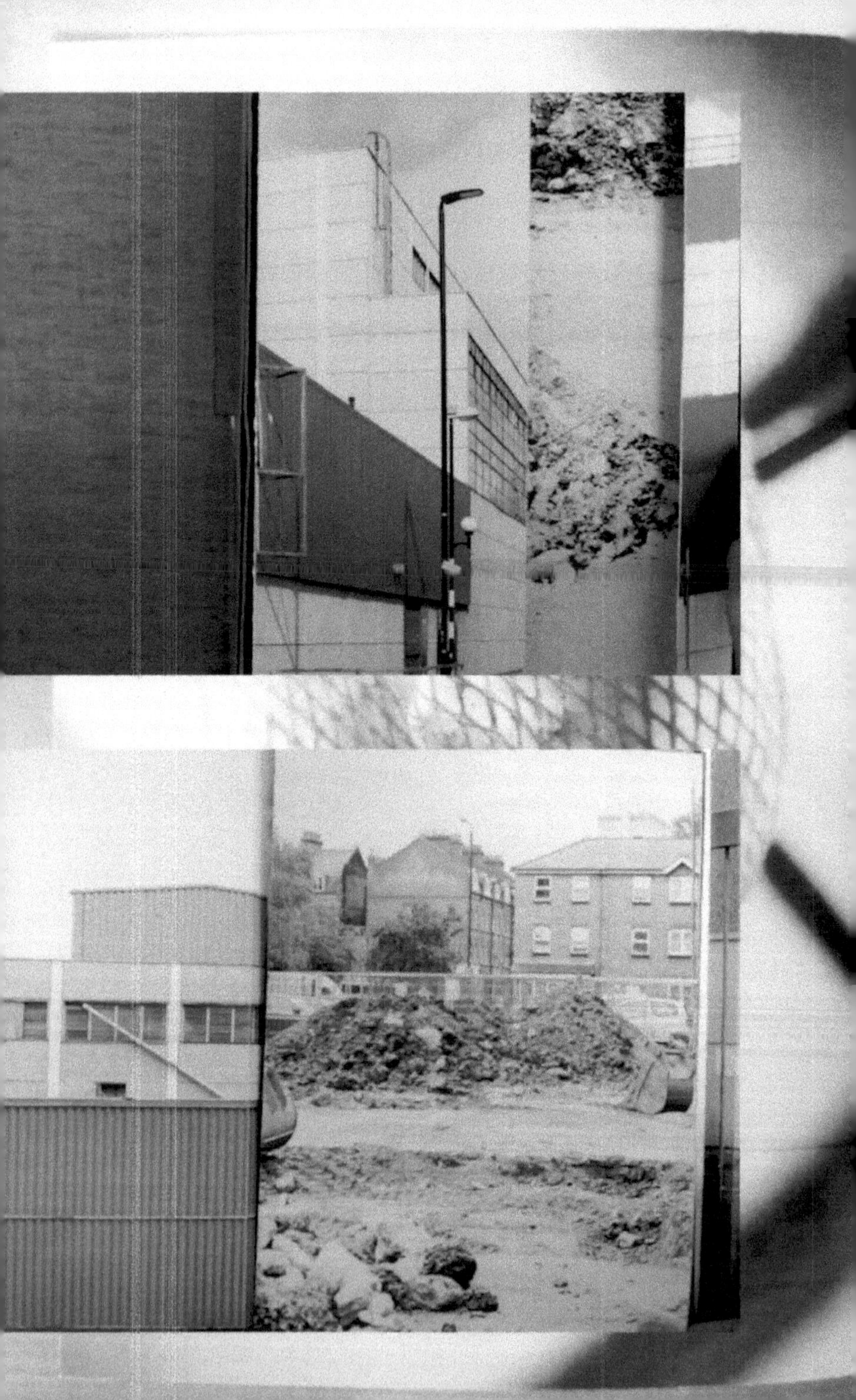

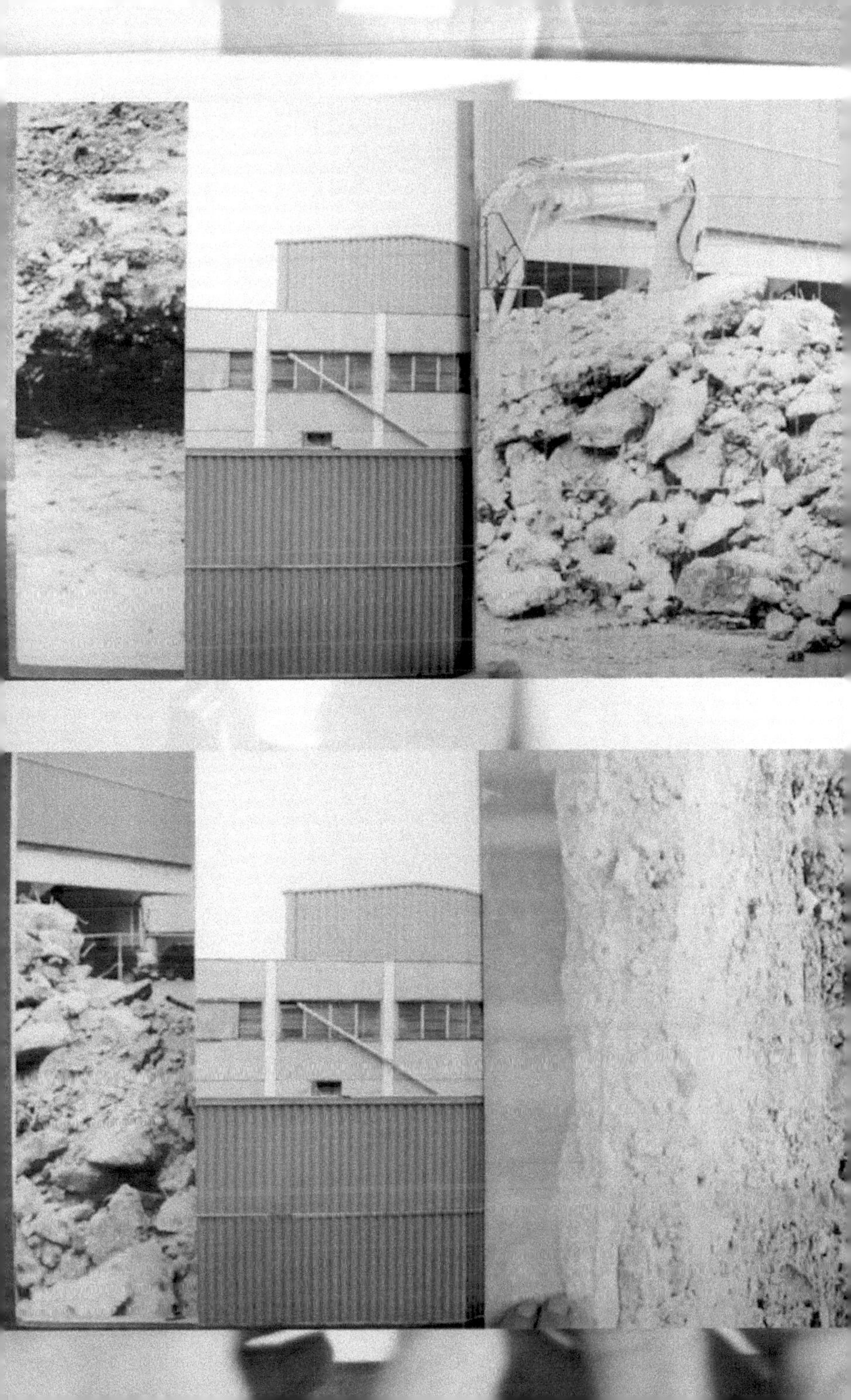

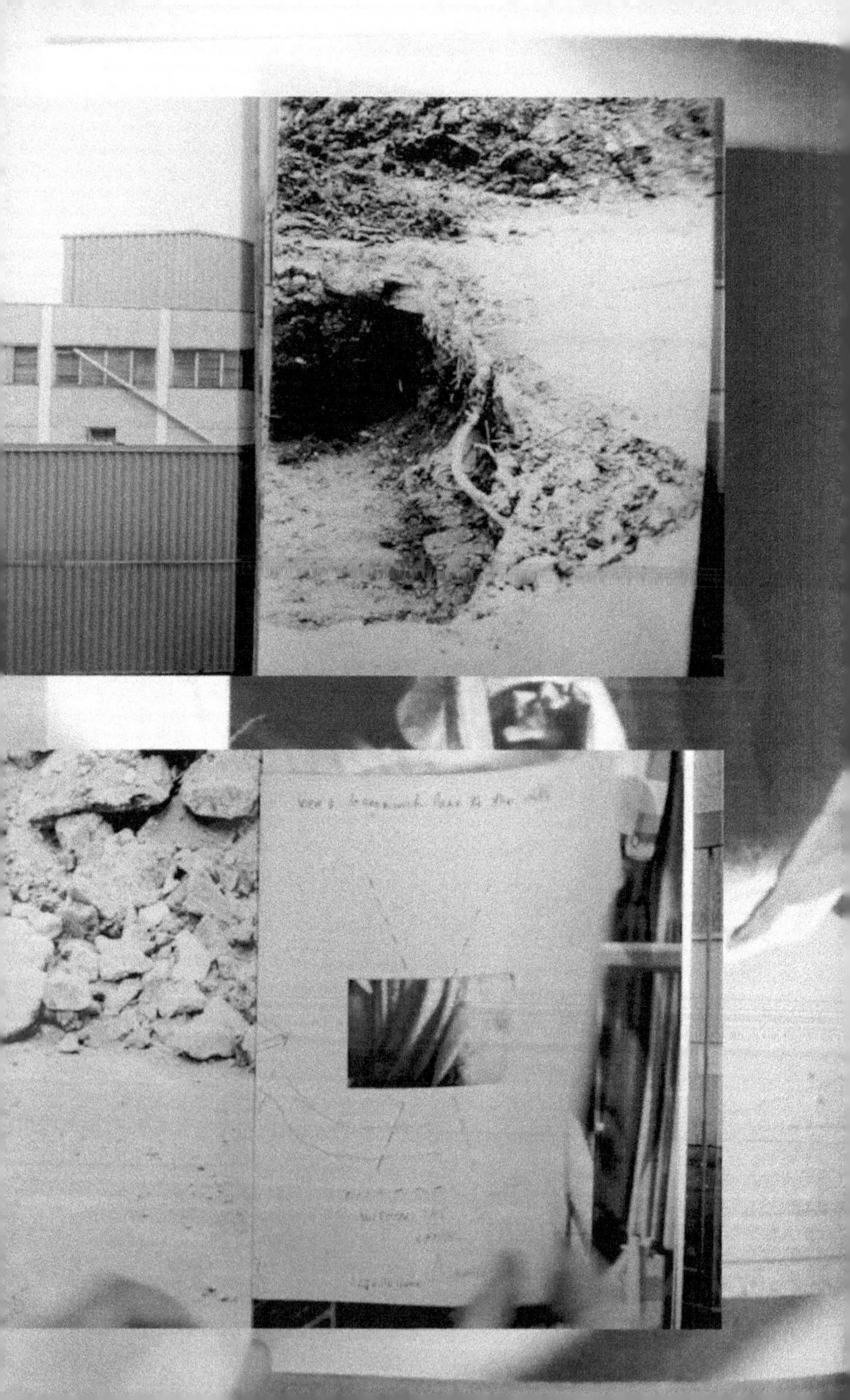

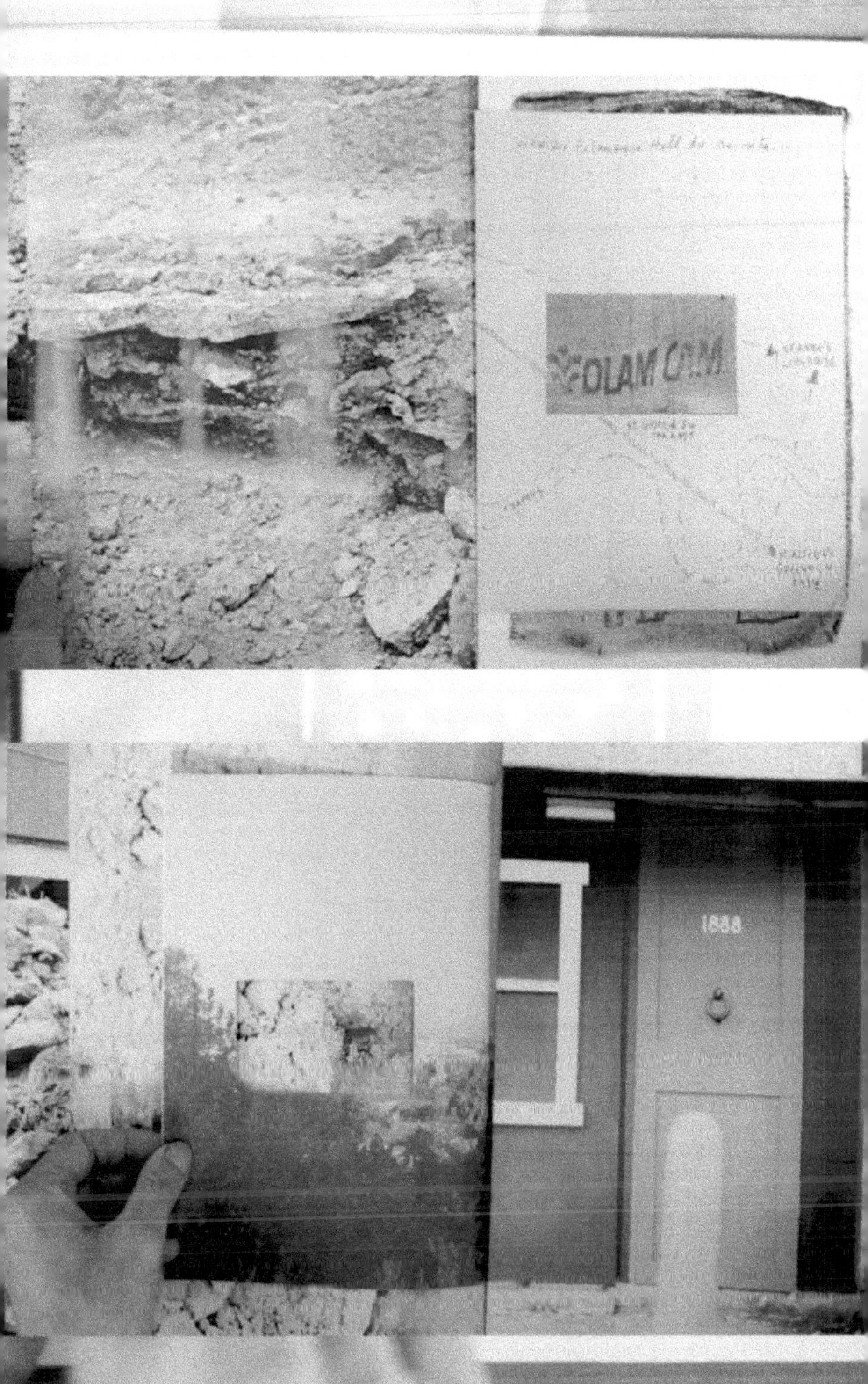
FOLAM O.M.
1888

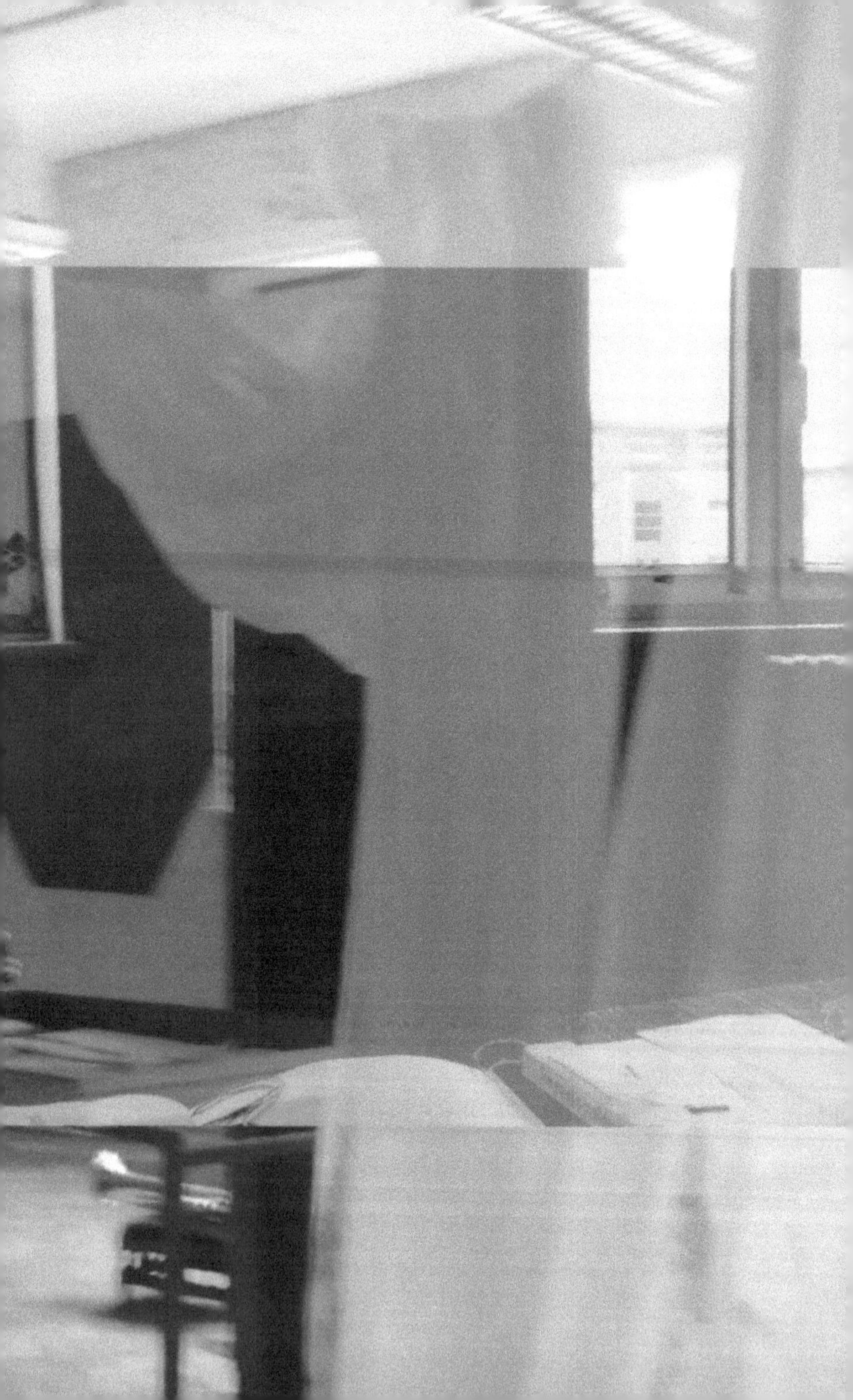

2.
The art of immersion: collection, research, display

Considering the experience of 'reading' the whole house–studio–gallery (and the 'constellations' of materials installed within it) is similar to reading a book. What we aim to investigate in this chapter is whether the occupation of the building – and the totality of paula's method that we call 'immersive' – has a visual structure similar to a book.

In this regard, it is necessary to ask the following questions:

Can paula's entire life and work process be incorporated into one single method?

Is all her activity and artistic production guided by the same principles?

Can we find the principles that guide her practice?

Could her method of living and working be analysed within the theoretical framework developed by Rancière?

Can we, within this analysis, identify the paradigmatic processes behind its functioning?

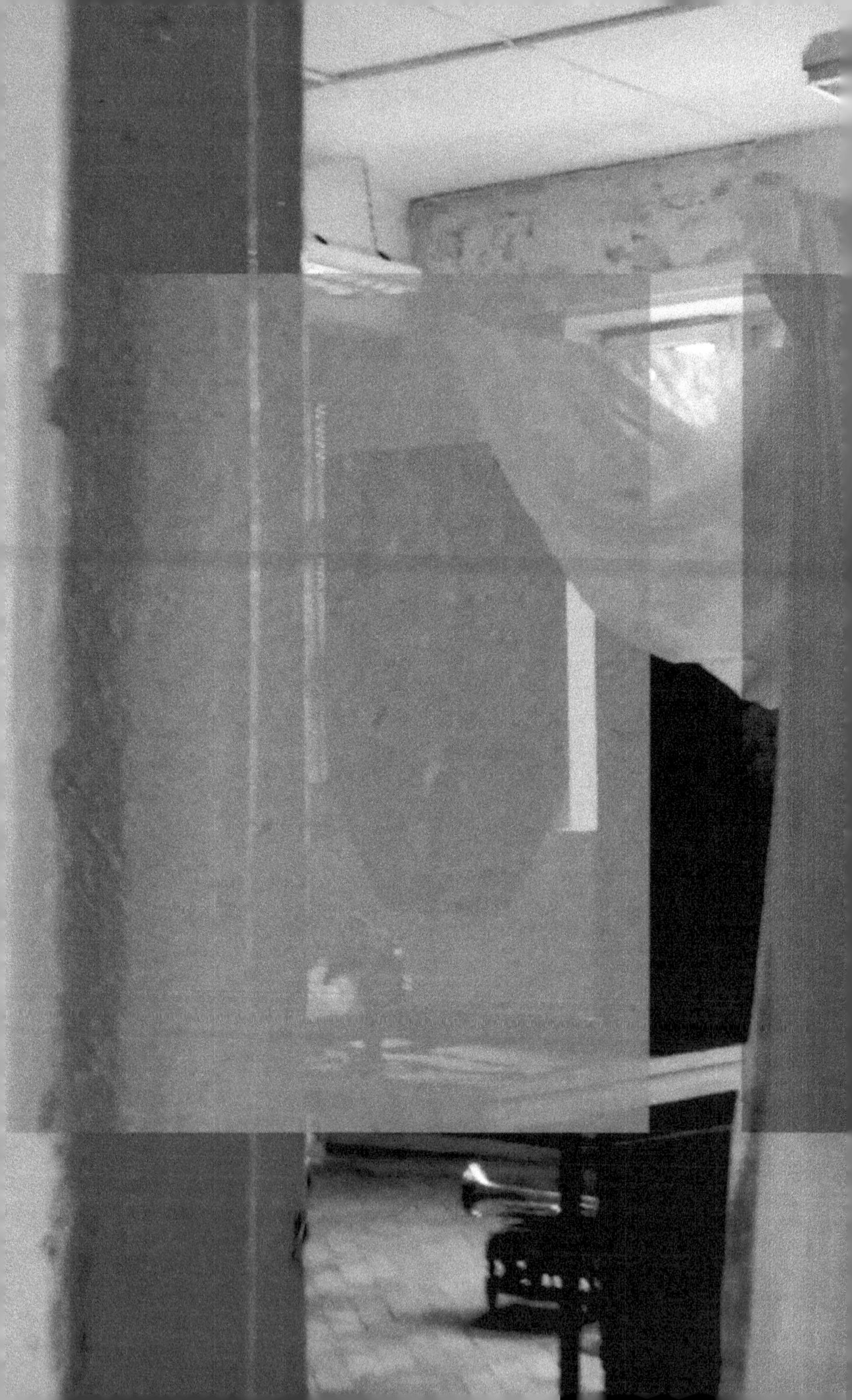

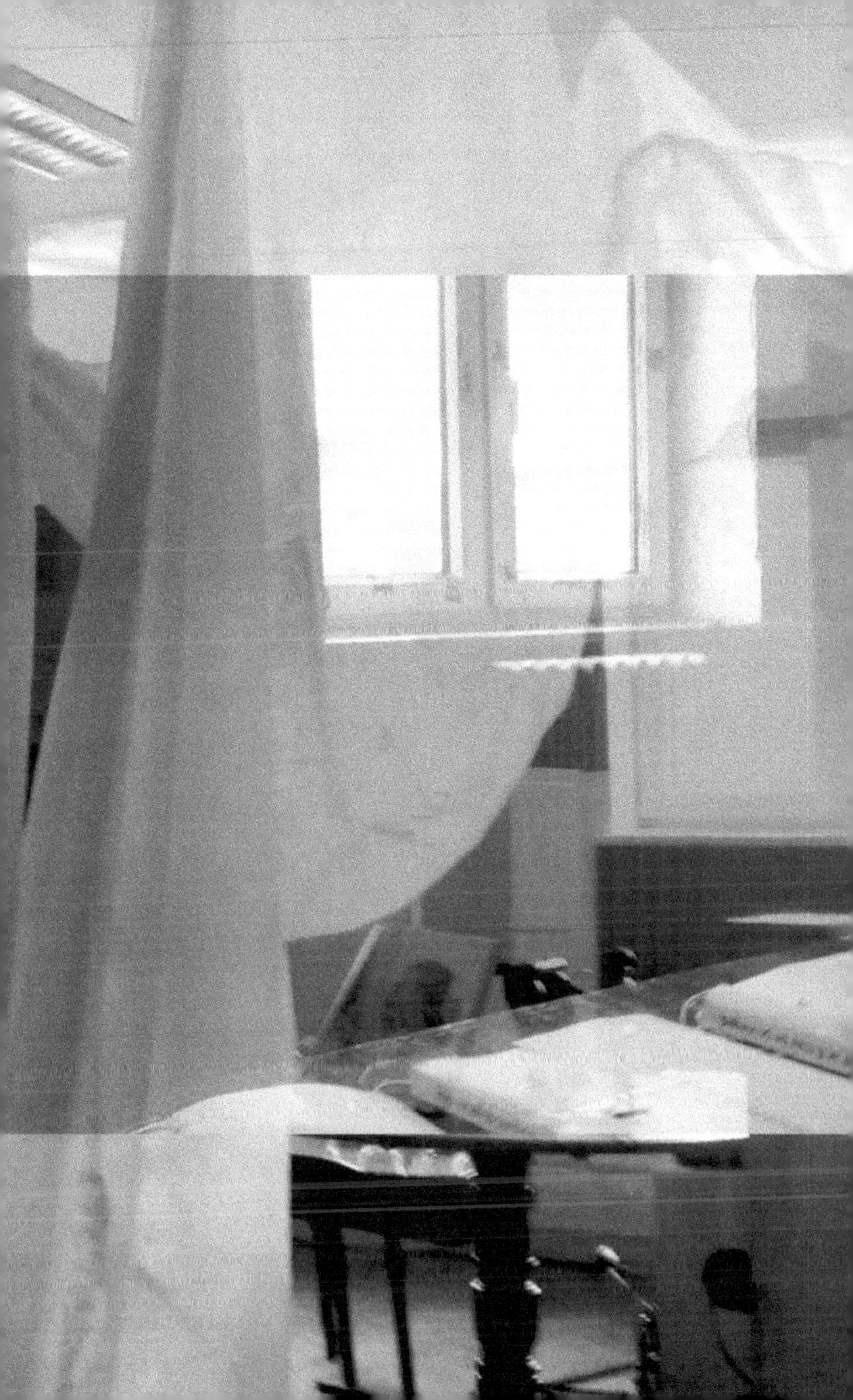

Immersion

As we have seen before, paula's main concern is her immersion in the places where she lives and where she sources materials from. These materials are investigated in their context, history, provenance and relationship to the commu-nity, as well as in relationship to the tripartite use she makes of the site, where living space is indistin-guishable from studio and exhibi-tion spaces.

This practice assumes the charac-teristics of an 'autoethnography,' and although the methods of this immersion process vary according to the location, there is always a simultaneous redefinition of her identity. The artefacts created as a result of this process— installations and objects—are transient, existing in a state of permanent mutability.

Mutability is transparent in paula's spaces because there is no distinction between private and public space, since there is no clear separation between spaces dedicated to daily life and exhibition spaces. Likewise, there is no separation between studio space and exhibition space (as we have already mentioned). Therefore it is not clearly distinguishable which materials are in a state of 'raw materials' or in a state of 'completed works.'

Add to this the constant recombination of the exhibited

artefacts, whose materials are permanently moved between 'collections' (agglomerations of materials or 'sandwiches of materials' and personal files) and books, and vice versa.

The analysis of paula's live-work context that I presented previously as 'immersion,' as well as her guiding principles will now be queried at the light of the theoretical framework assembled by Jacques Rancière in two of his books *The Future of the Image*[15] and *The Emancipated Spectator,*[16] as well as the *Glossary of Technical Terms* written by Gabriel Rockhill, published as an appendix

15 Jacques Ranciere, *The future of the Image*, (London: Verso, 2007).

16 Jacques Ranoiere, *The emancipated spectator*, (London: Verso, 2009)

to *The Politics of Aesthetics - The Distribution of the Sensible.*[17]

I will use the work titled <u>Blackchapel</u> as my case study to illustrate the process of immersion I previously analysed in a more general way. Using the concept of 'immersion' and this particular example as starting points, I will highlight three key operations of this method — collection, research and display of materials — and investigate whether the notion of 'dispositif' advanced by Rancière is suitable to describe these operations and paula's artistic processes.

17 Gabriel Rockhill, "Appendix I: Glossary of Technical Terms," In Jacques Ranciere, *The Politics of Aesthetics- The Distribution of the Sensible*, (London and New York: Bloomsbury Academic, 2013), 83-98.

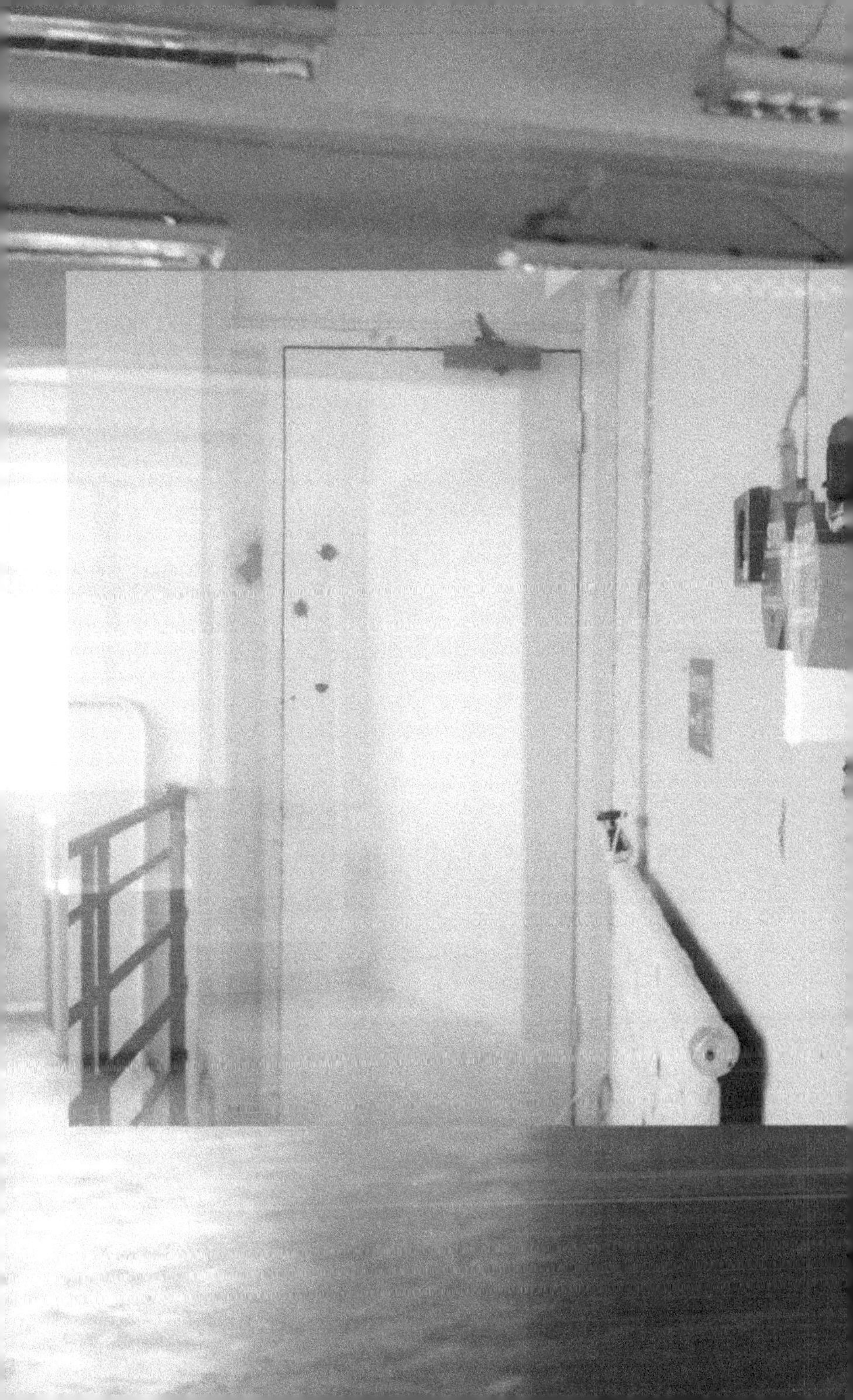

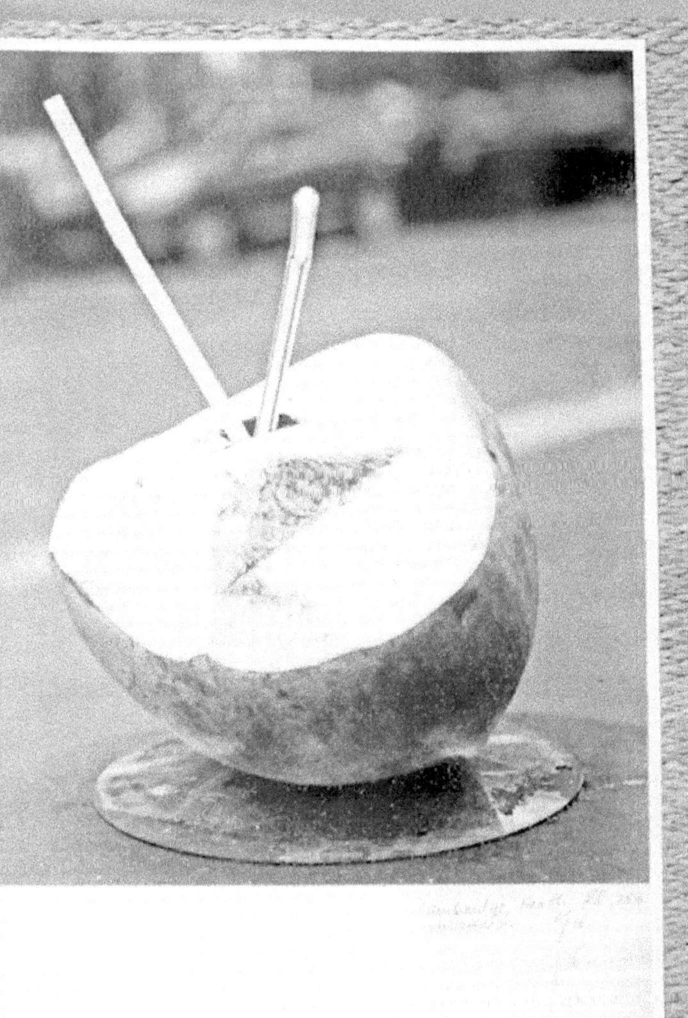

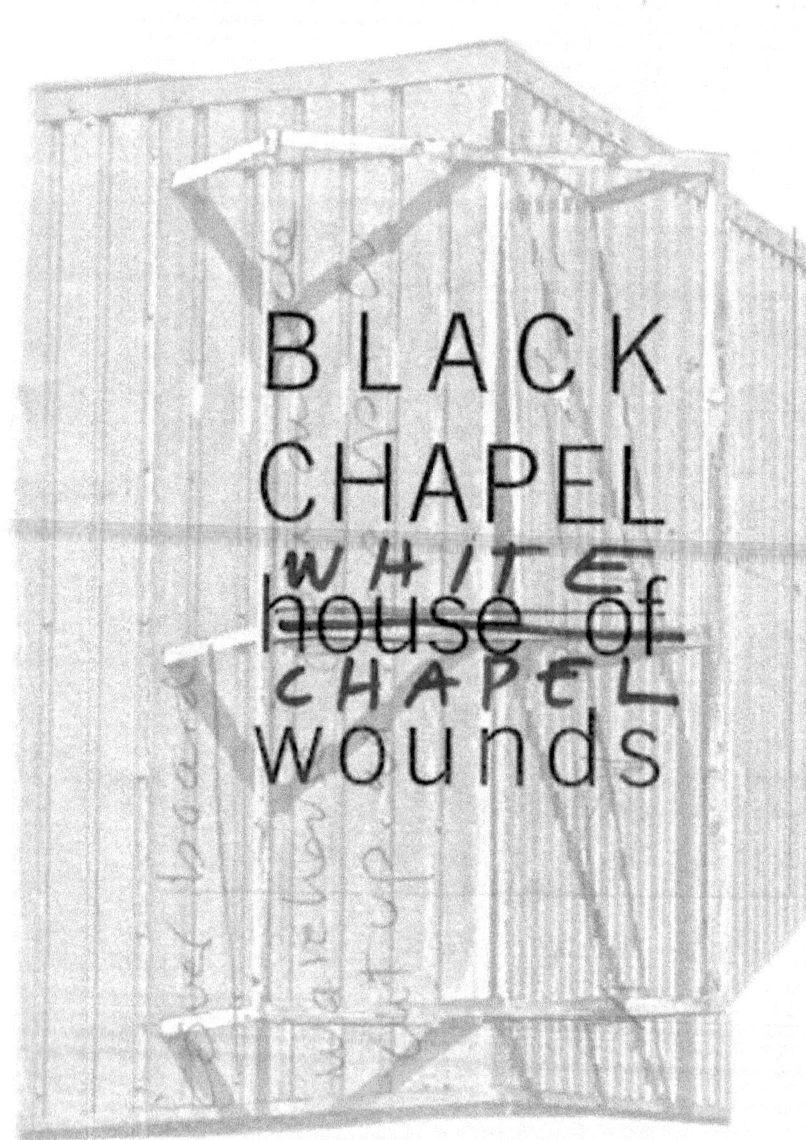

BLACK
CHAPEL
WHITEr
house of
CHAPEL
wounds

Dispositifs

I propose to analyse here whether paula's method of immersion and its key operations — identified as i) collection ii) research, and iii) display of materials — may be equated with 'dispositifs,' in the sense that Rancière gives them. That is, are these operating processes the same as 'dispositifs'?

Perhaps we can equate those three operations — collection, research and display of materials — to the articulation that Rancière, in the words of Rockhill,[18] makes between three things: ways of doing, their respective

18 Gabriel Rockhill, "Regimes of art (Les Régimes de l'art), Appendix I: Glossary of Technical Terms," in Jacques Rancière, *The Politics of Aesthetics- The Distribution of the Sensible* (London and New York: Bloomsbury Academic, 2013), 95.

forms of visibility, and ways of conceptualising both.

Following this approach, we will try to equate the three operations of 'immersion' to what Rancière calls 'a regime of art.'

A medium is not a 'proper' means or material. It is a surface of conversion: a surface of equivalence between the different arts' ways of making; a conceptual space of articulation between these ways of making and forms of visibility and intelligibility determining the way in which they can be viewed and conceived.[19]

It is noted that Rancière attributes an operational sense to

19 Jacques Rancière, *The future of the Image*, (London: Verso, 2007), 75.

'ways of doing' when delimiting the medium's field of attraction, he refers to it as a surface of conversion or equivalence between the ways of doing (which we can designate as operations) and the different arts.

Rancière articulates these with the forms of visibility (which I identify with 'display'), this articulation being determinant to the way different arts can be seen and thought (which I identify with 'research'). We identify, thus, the three key operations of the immersive process with the operations that Rancière lists in his definition of medium.

But are these operations identifiable with 'dispositifs'? Let us quote Rancière again:

> *The point is not to counter-pose reality to its appearances. It is to construct different realities, different forms of common sense— that is to say, different spatiotemporal systems, different communities of words and things, form and meanings.*[20]

A 'dispositif' is, after all, a 'community' of linguistic elements that are objectual, formal and induce ways to perceive, to be affected by and attribute meaning.

It seems to me that 'dispositifs' are mechanisms that through

20 Jacques Rancière, *The emancipated spectator*, (London: Verso, 2009)

operations (ways of doing) conceptualise and make visible 'new communities' or new spaces *"of words and things, form and meanings."*

In other words, they create new circumstances for the elements and their meanings, which are, after all, what the key operations ('collection,' 'research' and 'display') of paula's operating method ('immersion') do.

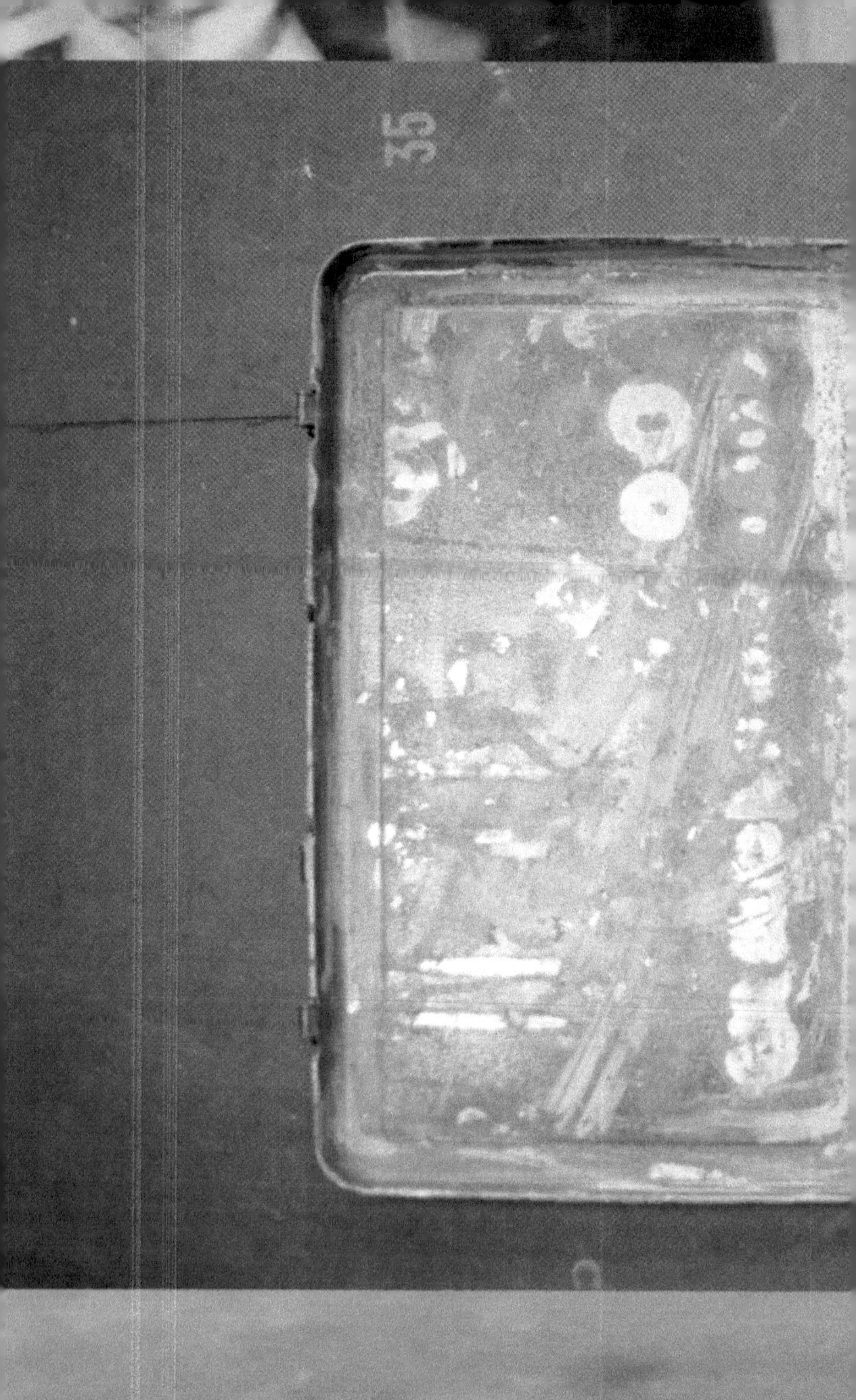

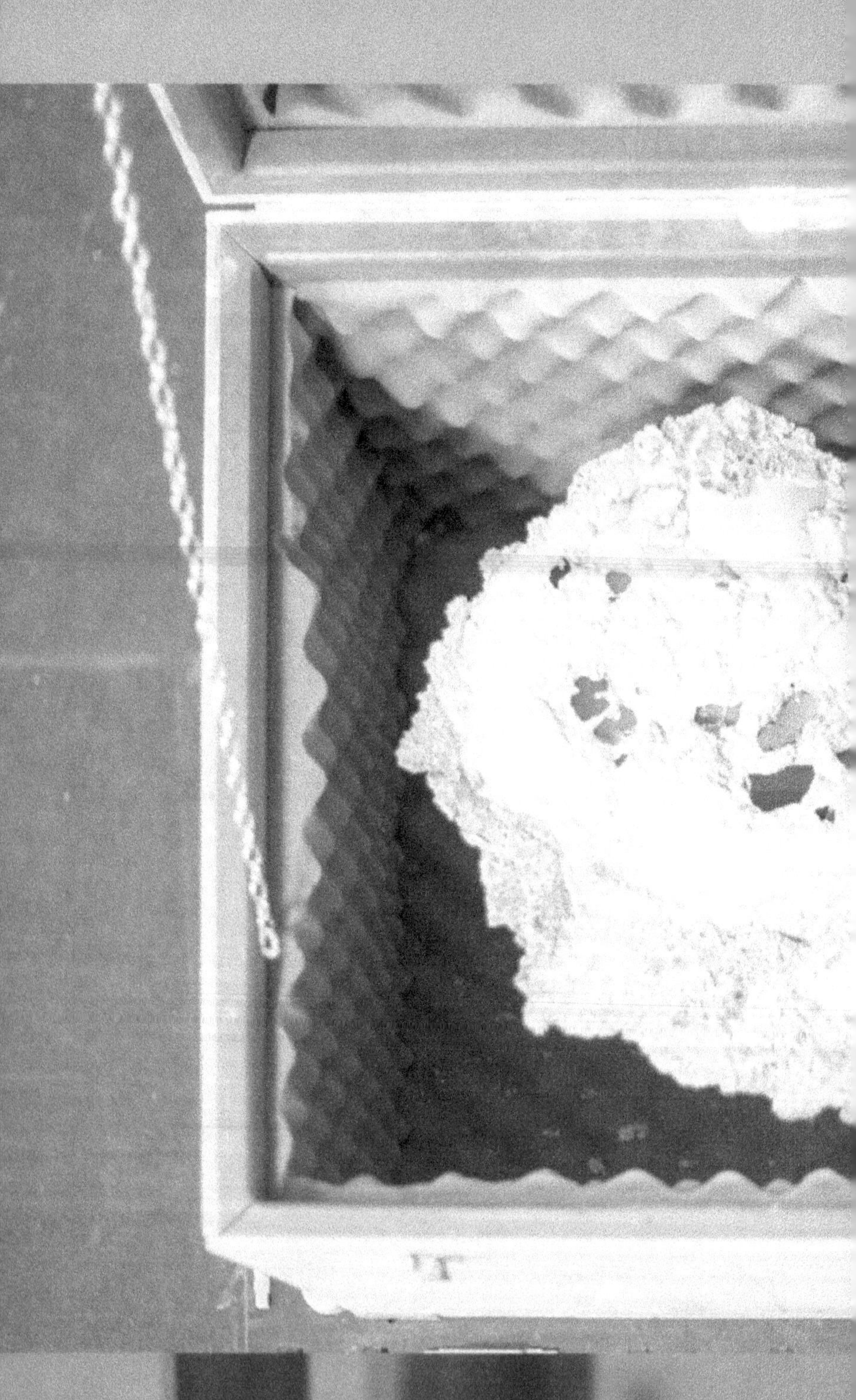

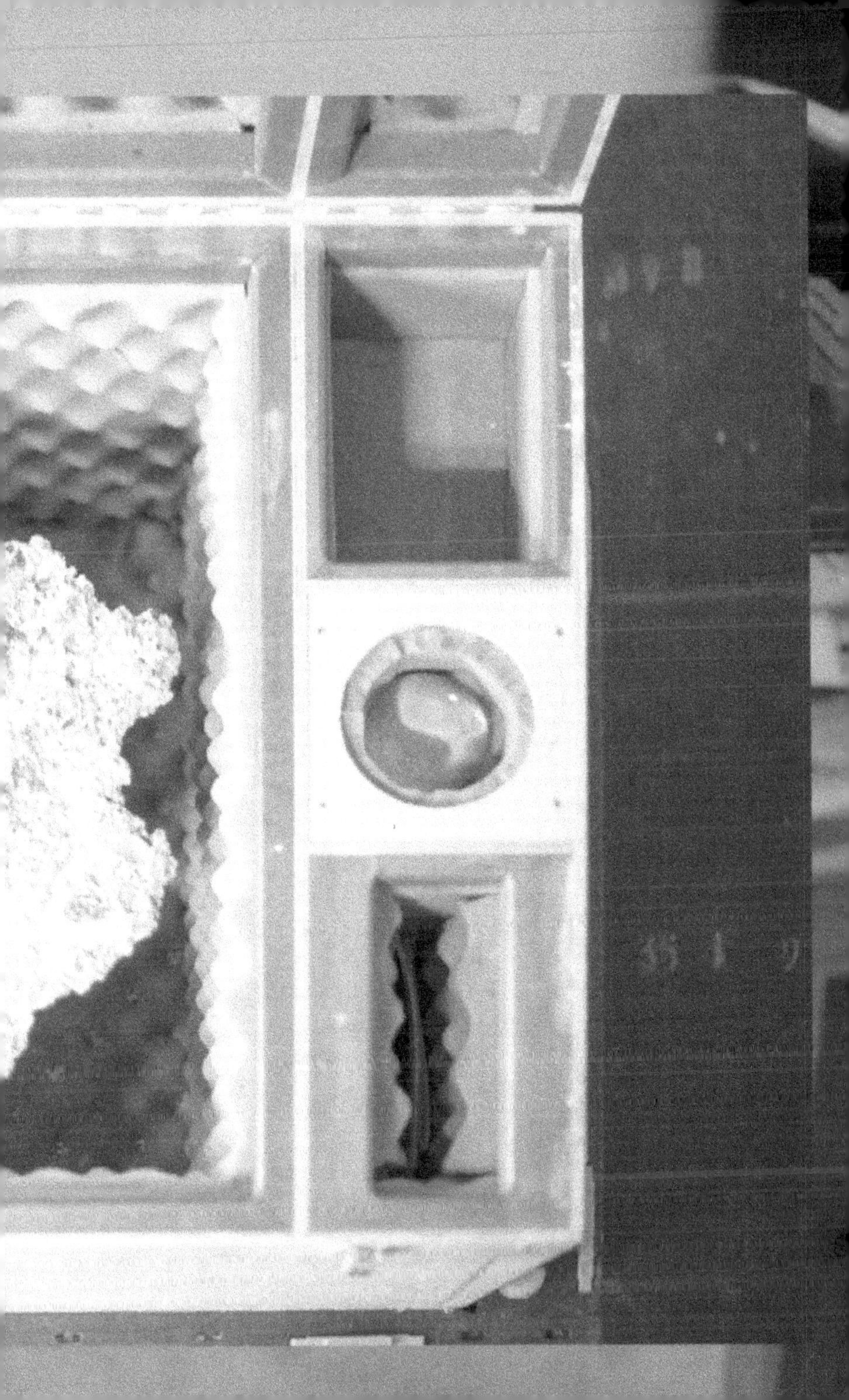

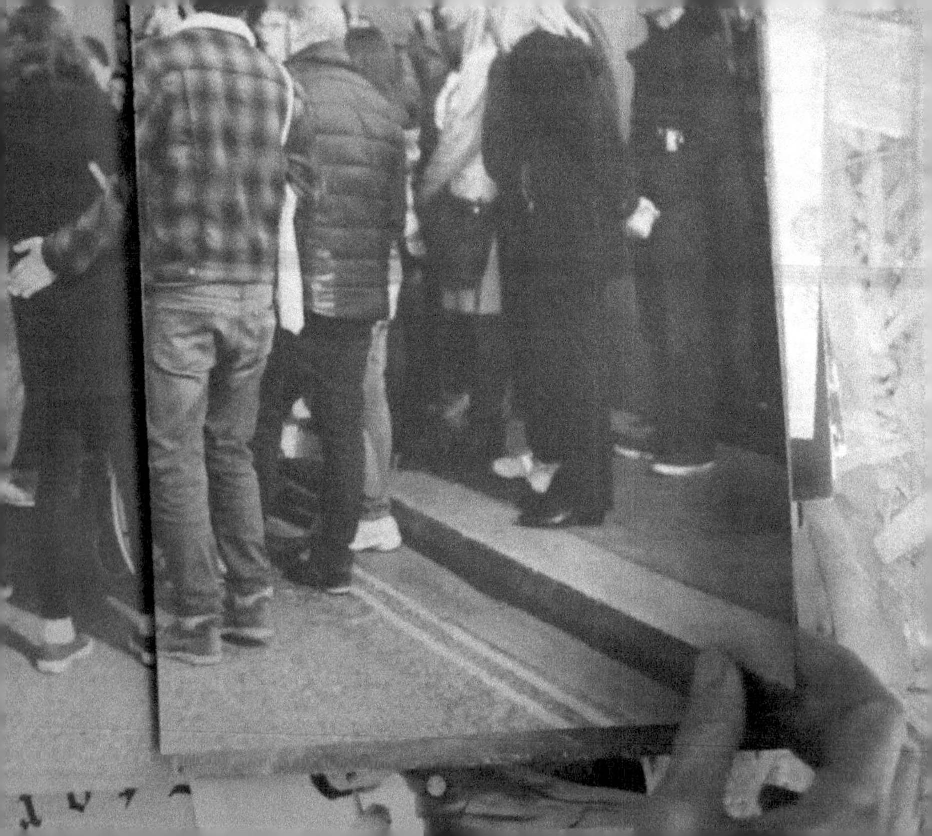

The
world
puts its
stock
in us.℠

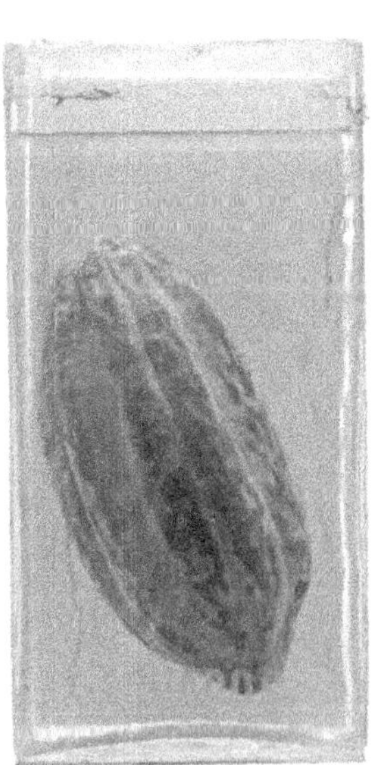

OT N° KKCI 1151/ASCI/2014

HDV Sarl

L'Habitude de Vérifier
18 BP 1240 Abidjan 18
Tél.: 21 24 58 00
Fax : 21 24 32 62

ECHANTILLON MOYEN

Exportateur	Africa sourcing
Site	SKV
Marque	Africa sourcing
Nombre de sacs	3460
N° du lot	R1
Date de sondage	09 / 03 / 2015

Dispositif I: Collection

Upon her arrival in Whitechapel, paula notes that *"I started to realise that there were structural elements of the Whitechapel experience which were elements of alienation in relation to space."*[21] paula's perception of the space to which she moved (both the building and its context) provided her, as we have already seen, with an opportunity to work through her *"own emotions related to the space,"* which began with the collection of materials from her surrounding environment. These were installed on site, operating a rearrangement of

21 Face-to face conversation with paula roush (msdm house-studio-gallery, London), November 23, 2019.

her immediate context of life and artistic work, with new materials and in an interdependent form, a rearrangement of her personal identity data, developing a process similar to that expressed by Rancière:

> *The labour of art thus involves playing on the ambiguity of resemblances and the instability of dissemblances, bringing about a local reorganisation, a singular rearrangement of circulating images. In a sense the construction of such devices assigns art the task that once fell to the "critique of images."* [22]

For paula, these operations are, however, less 'modest,' more

22 Rancière, *The future of the Image*, 24.

'radical' and 'demystifying' than Rancière indicates as being characteristic of artists who do a *"critique of images,"* since according to him artists tend *"to dedicate their operations to more modest tasks."*[23]

In fact, for paula there is a recombination of materials according to affinities (dynamic or changeable) that she finds (in a permanent 'work in progress'), endowing the new agglomerations ('sandwiches,' clusters or 'constellations') with a more radical symbolic charge, I would say, than that Rancière attributes to artists' actions.

23 ibid, 24.

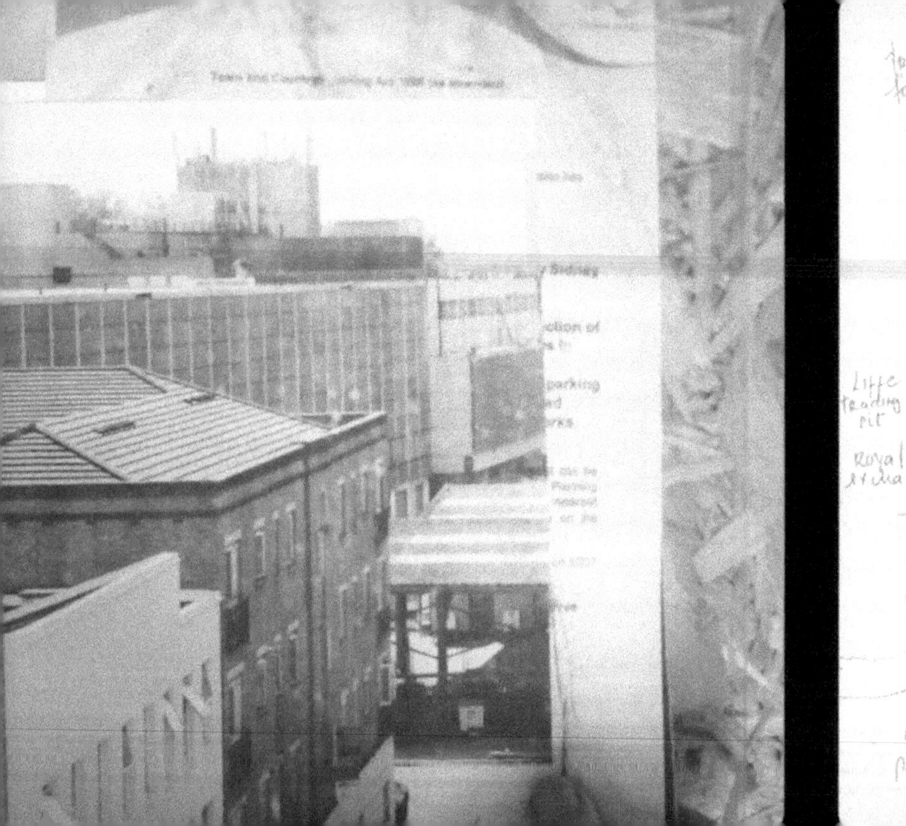

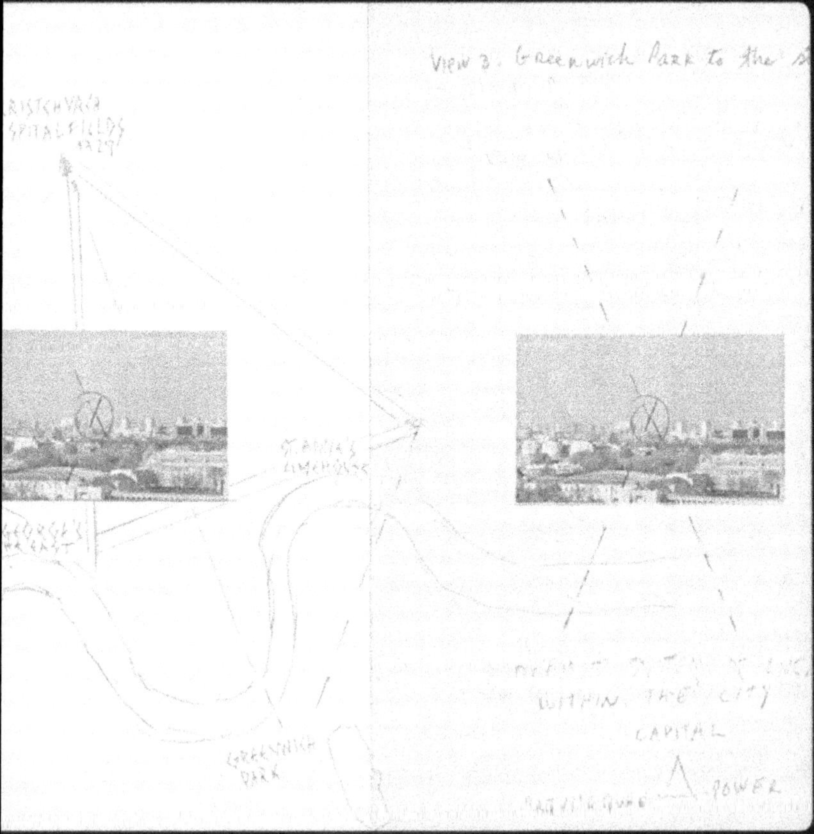

View 3. Greenwich Park to the s[t]

CHRISTCHURCH
SPITALFIELDS
1729

ST GEORGE'S
IN THE EAST

ST ANNE'S
LIMEHOUSE

GREENWICH
PARK

WITHIN THE CITY

CAPITAL

POWER

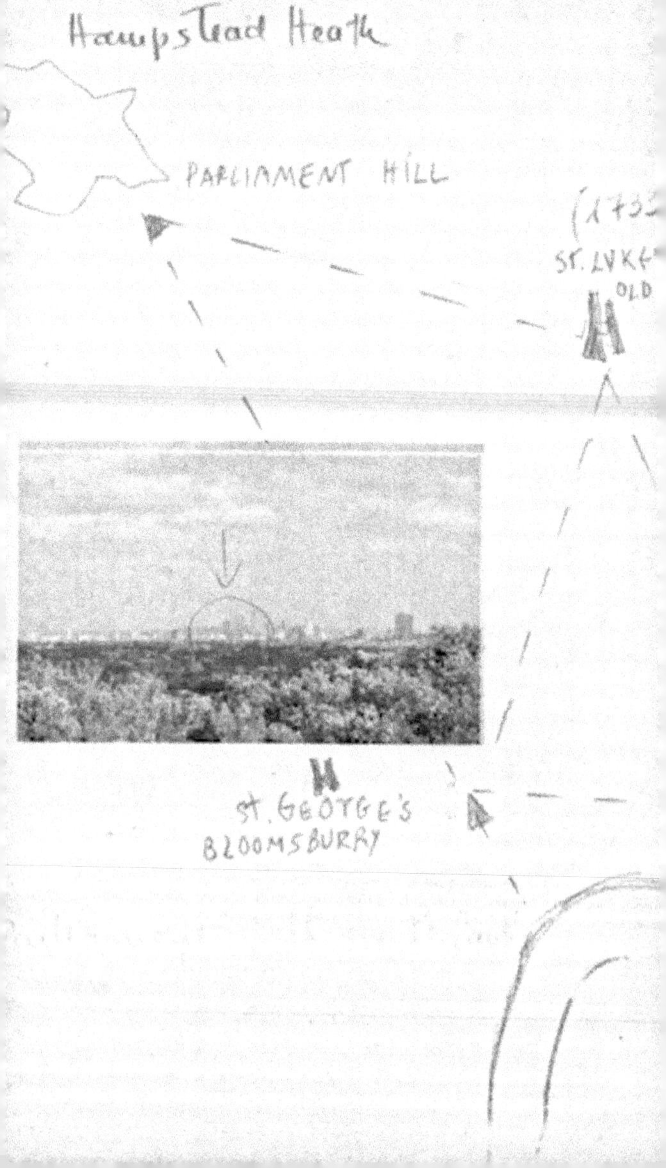

Hampstead Heath

PARLIAMENT HILL

(1733
ST. LUKE'S OLD

St. GEORGE'S
BLOOMSBURY

PARLIAMENT HILL

view 1: Parliament Hill to the
CHRISTCHURCH
SPITALFIELDS
ST. MARY'S
WOOLNOTH
ST. GEORGE'S
IN THE EAST
THAMES

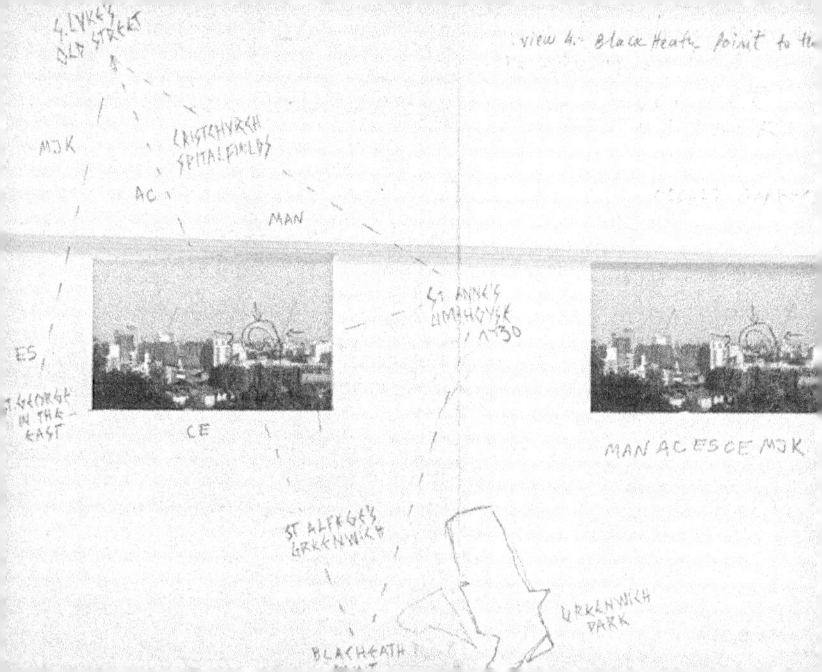

S. LUKES OLD STREET
view 4: Blackheath Point to th
MJK
CRISTCHURCH SPITALFIELDS
AC
MAN
ES
T GEORGE IN THE EAST
St ANNE'S LIMEHOUSE
↑~30
CE
MAN AC ES CE MJK
ST ALFEGE'S GREENWICH
GREENWICH PARK
BLACHEATH

Dispositif II: Research

The work of research and (re) signification of materials mobilised in _Blackchapel_ – photographs and artefacts constructed from contextual survey and archival research – constitute, as we have already seen, a process of 'contamination' that has an 'anachronistic dynamic.'

Thus, the structuring logic of this dispositif (the investigation) is not, as we have already seen, necessarily chronological, but of a different order, as is the case for example with the combination, in _Blackchapel,_ of the psycho-geographic survey of the area with the planning application for the site, a reality that paula translates by saying: *"I thought of articulating a discourse on the occult of Whitechapel, of which there is an extensive bibliography, with the psychogeography of East London and a photographic investigation of everyday urban space."*[24]

As we can see, there is no intention here of the literal and chronological transcription of a report, but rather, it is a work on the fissure of the representational 'disposif' that Rancière points out:

> *Thus, the problem does not concern the moral or political validity of the message transmitted by the*

24 Face-to-face conversation with paula

*representational dispositif.
It does concern the dispositif
itself. Its fissure shows that
the effectiveness of art is
not to transmit messages,
provide models or decipher
representations.*[25]

That is, it is about finding other structuring logics that result from the rearrangement of the materials mobilised, researched and constructed. A process that Rancière formulates as follows:

*It consists first of all of the
dispositions of the bodies,
it consists of the cut-out of
spaces and singular times that
define ways of being together
or separately, facing or in the*

25 Jacques Rancière, *O Espectador emancipado*, (Lisboa: Orfeu Negro, 2010), 83. Translation by the author.

middle of, inside or outside, in proximity or at a distance.[26]

And this is because in the action of this 'dispositif' there is no linearity between cause and effect. As Rancière explains, there is no

> *sensible continuity between, on the one hand, the production of images, gestures or words, and, on the other, the perception of a situation that compromises the spectators' thoughts, feelings and actions.*[27]

26 Ibid, 83.

27 Ibid, 82.

Dispositif III: display

The 'display' — or what appears to us as 'complete works' — is not, as I have already pointed out, a final state. See what paula says about <u>Blackchapel</u>'s 'display': *"It is on several tables because now I'm trying to resolve it as an installation."*[28]

Its condition is recombinatory, always transitory, and can, in a circular process, return to the condition of 'raw materials.' Because, as already explained, collections ('sandwiches,' installations and agglomerations) and books — what constitutes the 'display ' — share with the building this condition of being a space

–time sequence, and a narrative structure.

The movement of transformation of the 'display' is inherent to the construction of narratives: of objects, space and the entire process of immersion.

We can identify in this narrative 'disposif' of 'display' an 'aesthetic efficacy' that, being grounded in its unpredictable mutability, challenges any fixed relationship between creative production and a *"determined effect on a specific audience."*[29] Since, as this is the case, *"a critical art is an art that knows that its political effect happens through an aesthetic distance."*[30]

29 Rancière, *O Espectador emancipado*, 88. Translation by the author.

30 Ibid, 122.

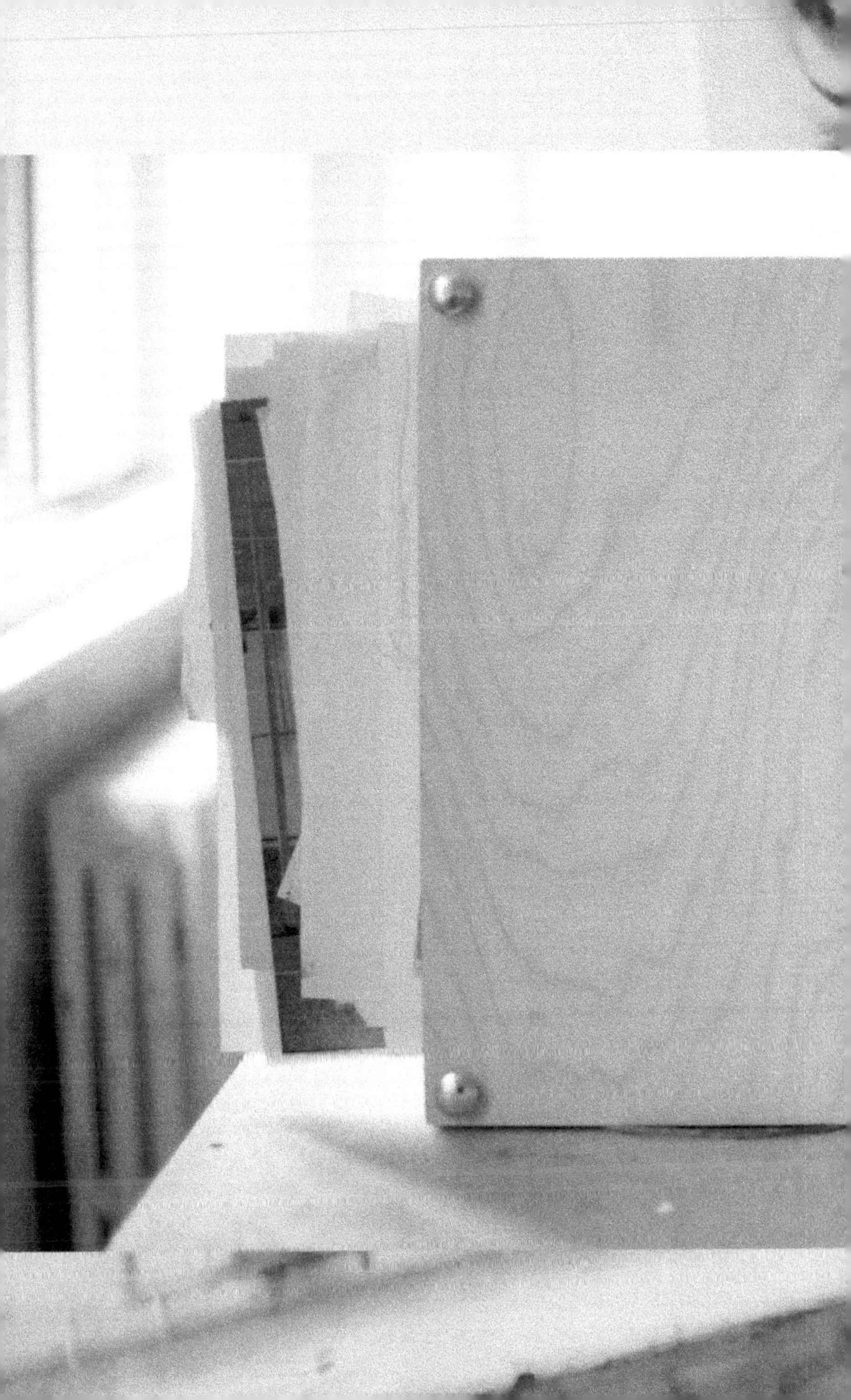

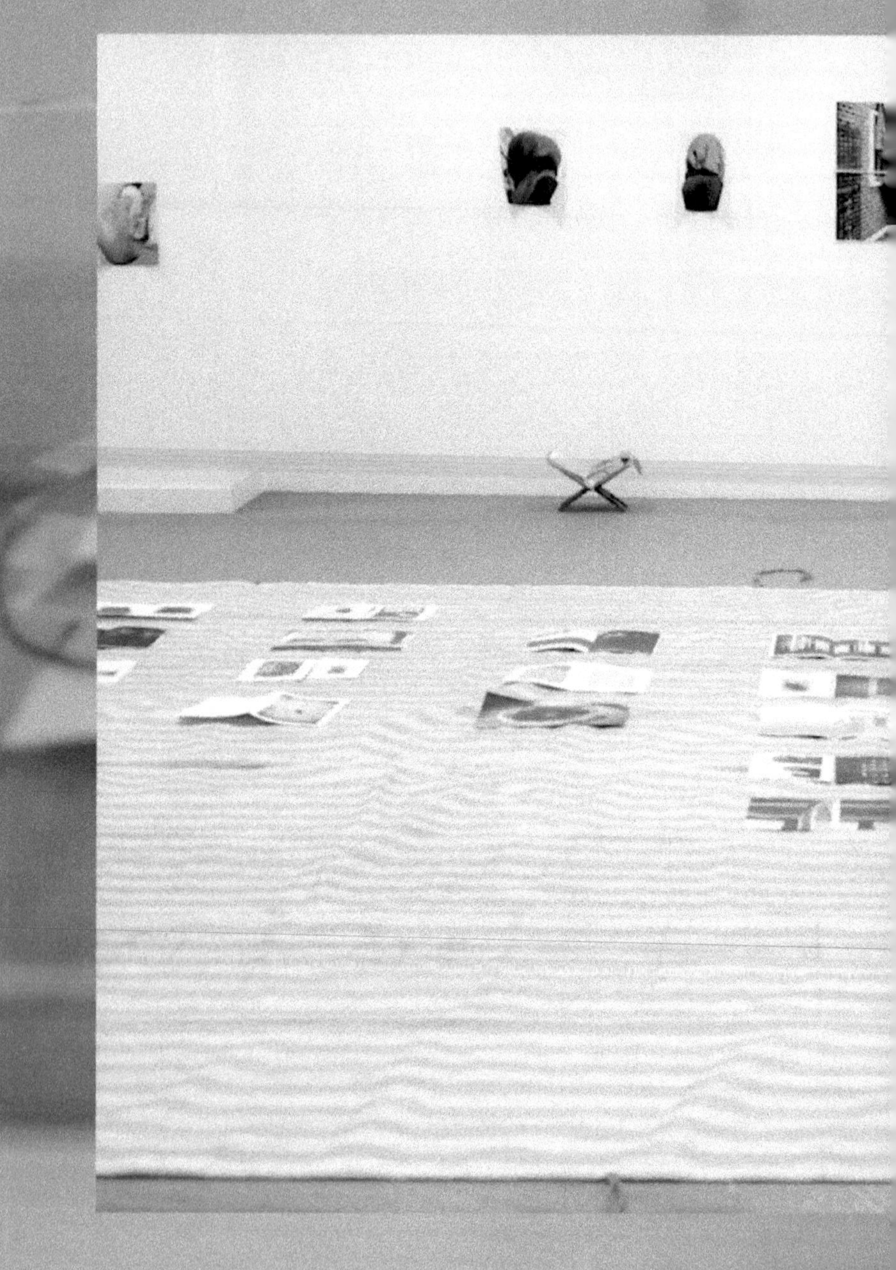

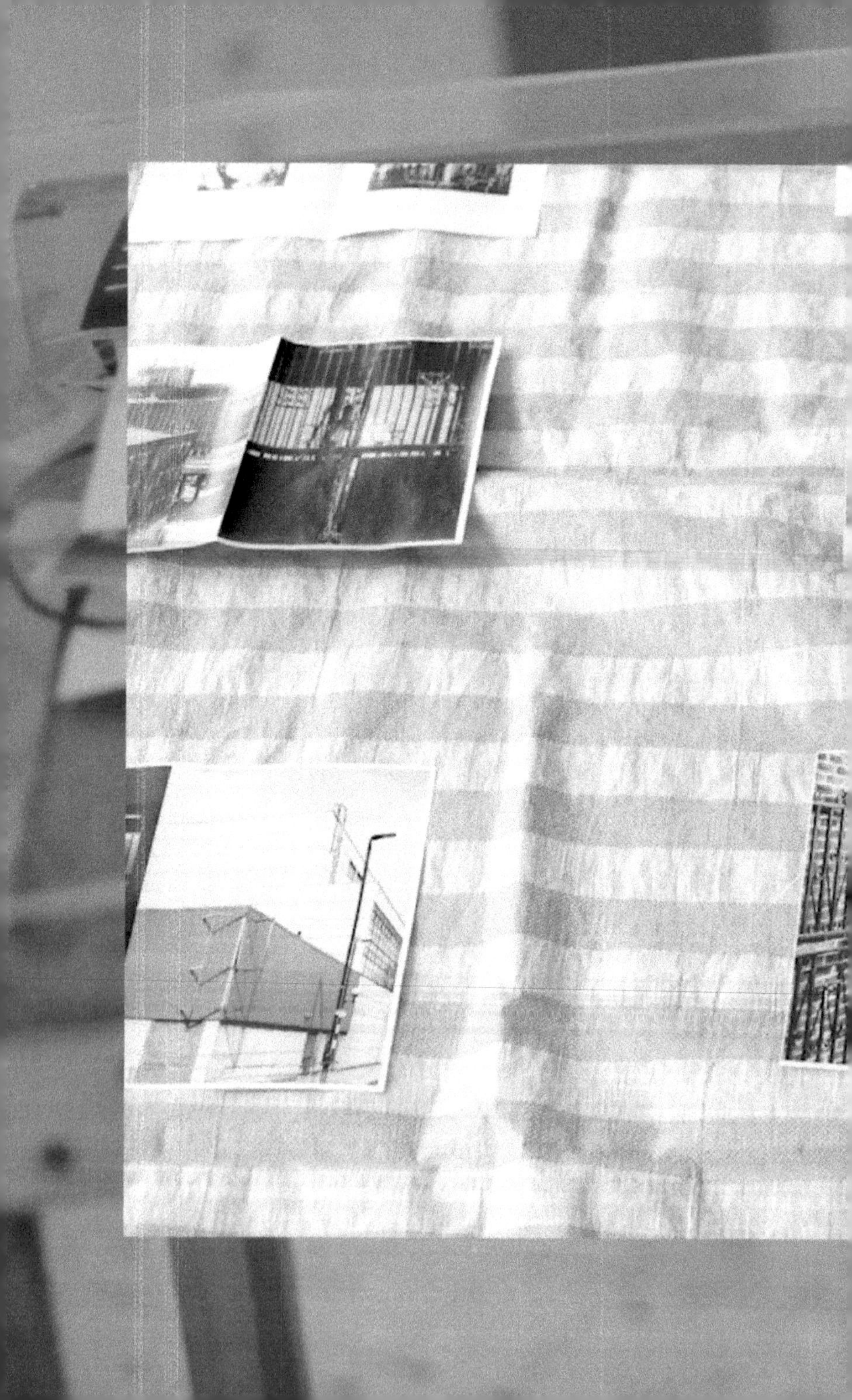

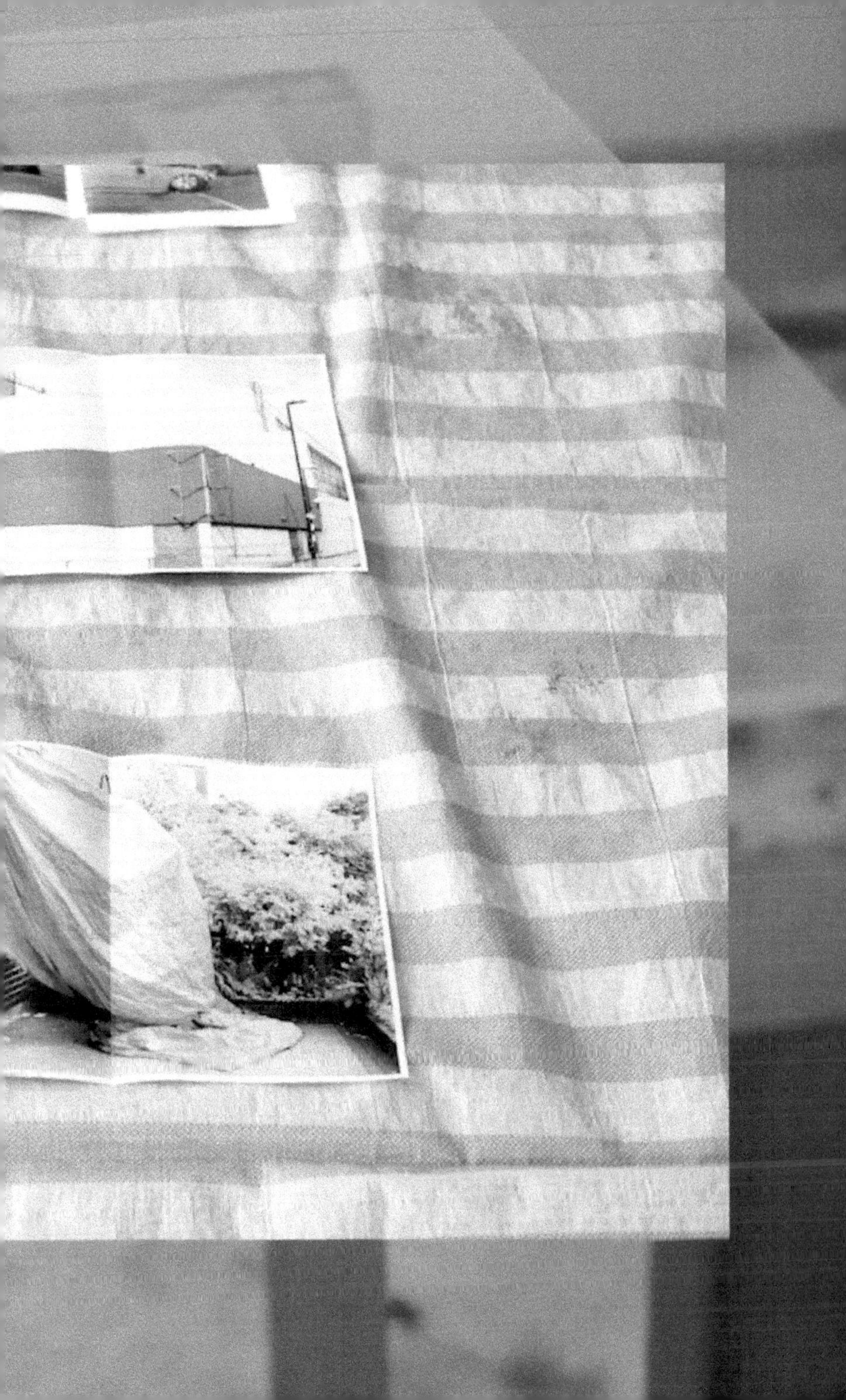

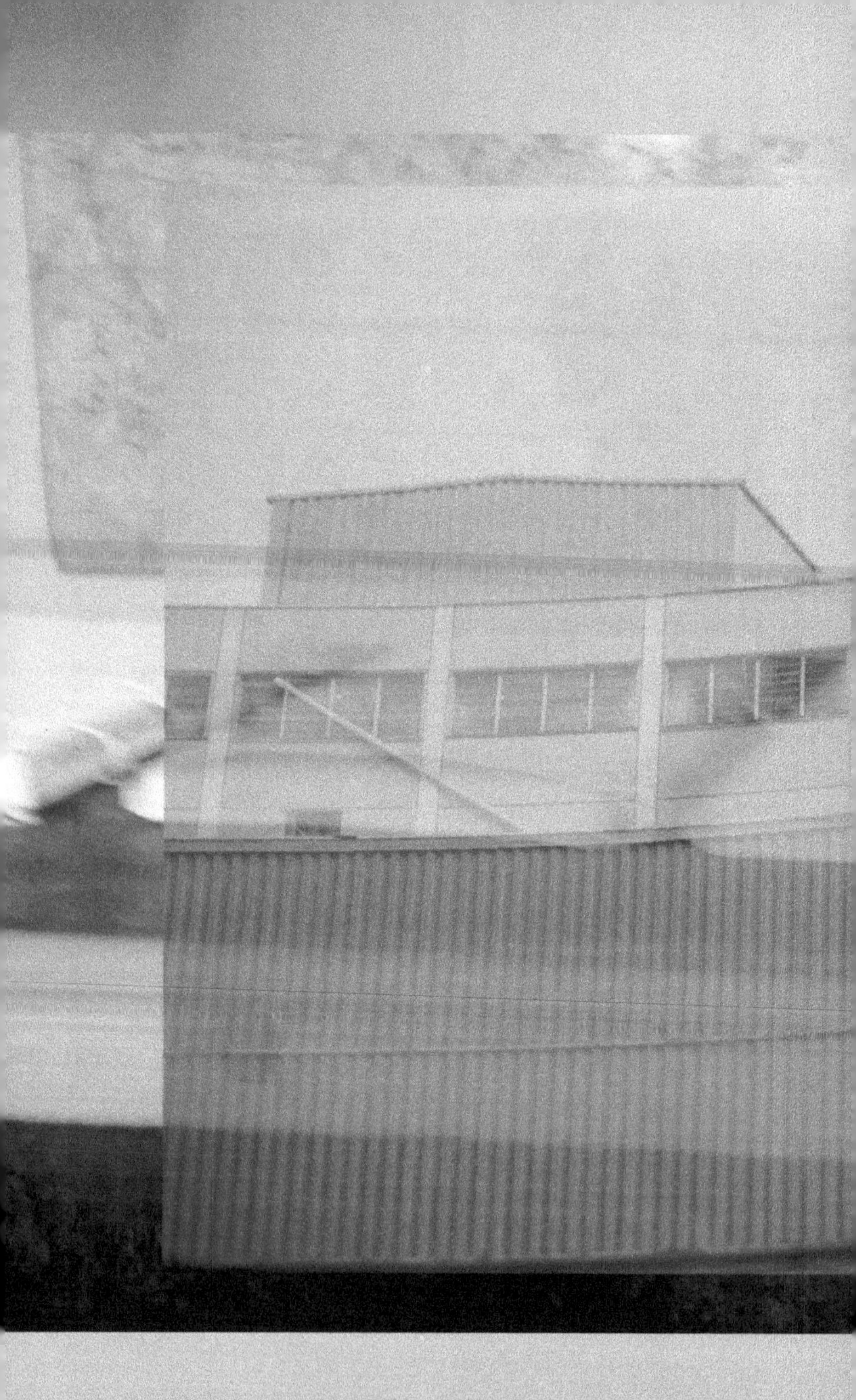

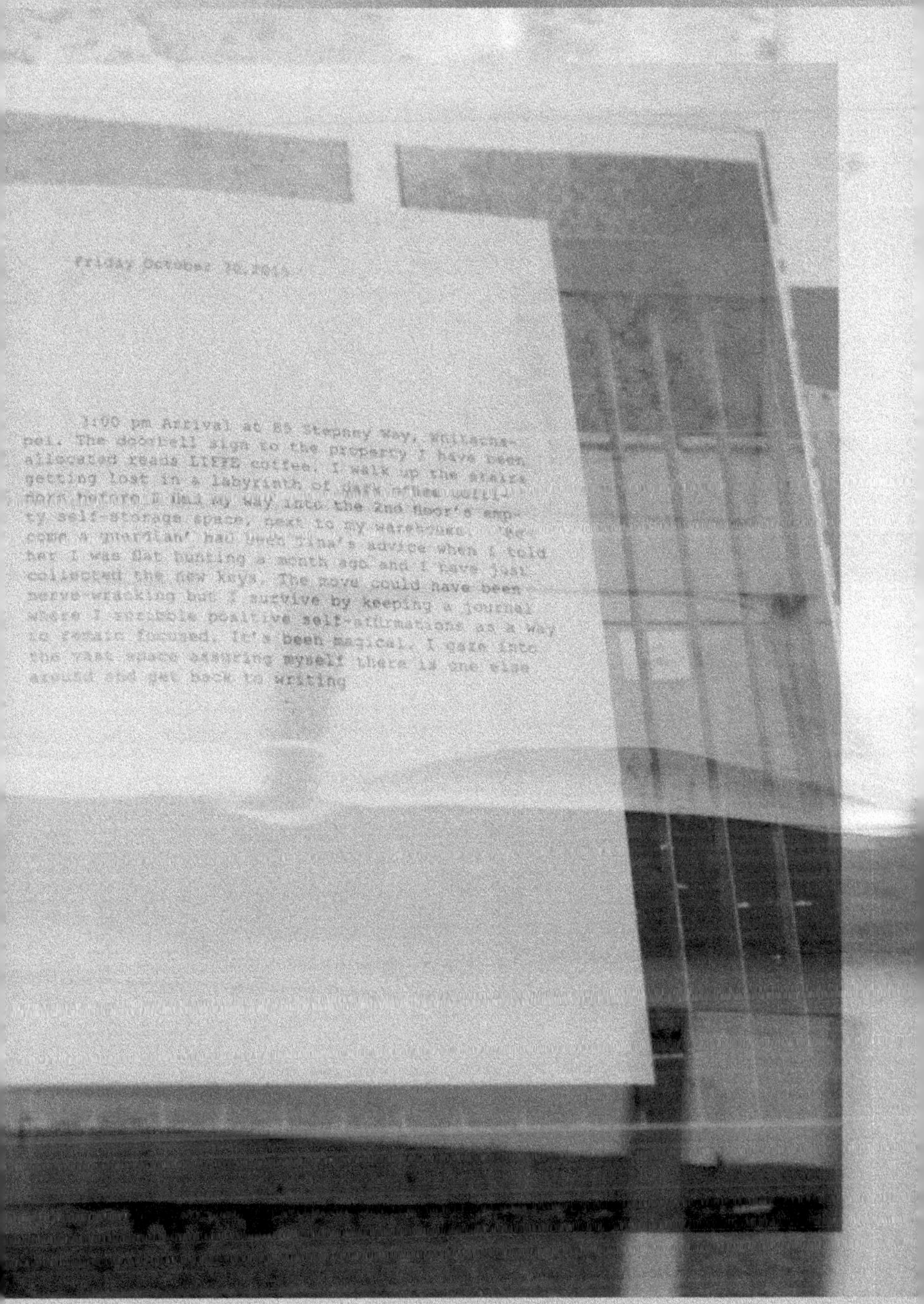

1:00 pm Arrival at 85 Stepney Way, Whitechapel. The doorbell sign to the property I have been allocated reads LIFFE coffee. I walk up the stairs dark before I find my way into the 2nd floor's empty self-storage space, next to my warehouse. 'Become a guardian' had been Tina's advice when I told her I was flat hunting a month ago and I have just collected the new keys. The move could have been nerve-wracking but I survive by keeping a journal where I scribble positive self-affirmations as a way to remain focused. It's been magical. I gaze into the vast space assuring myself there is one else around and get back to writing

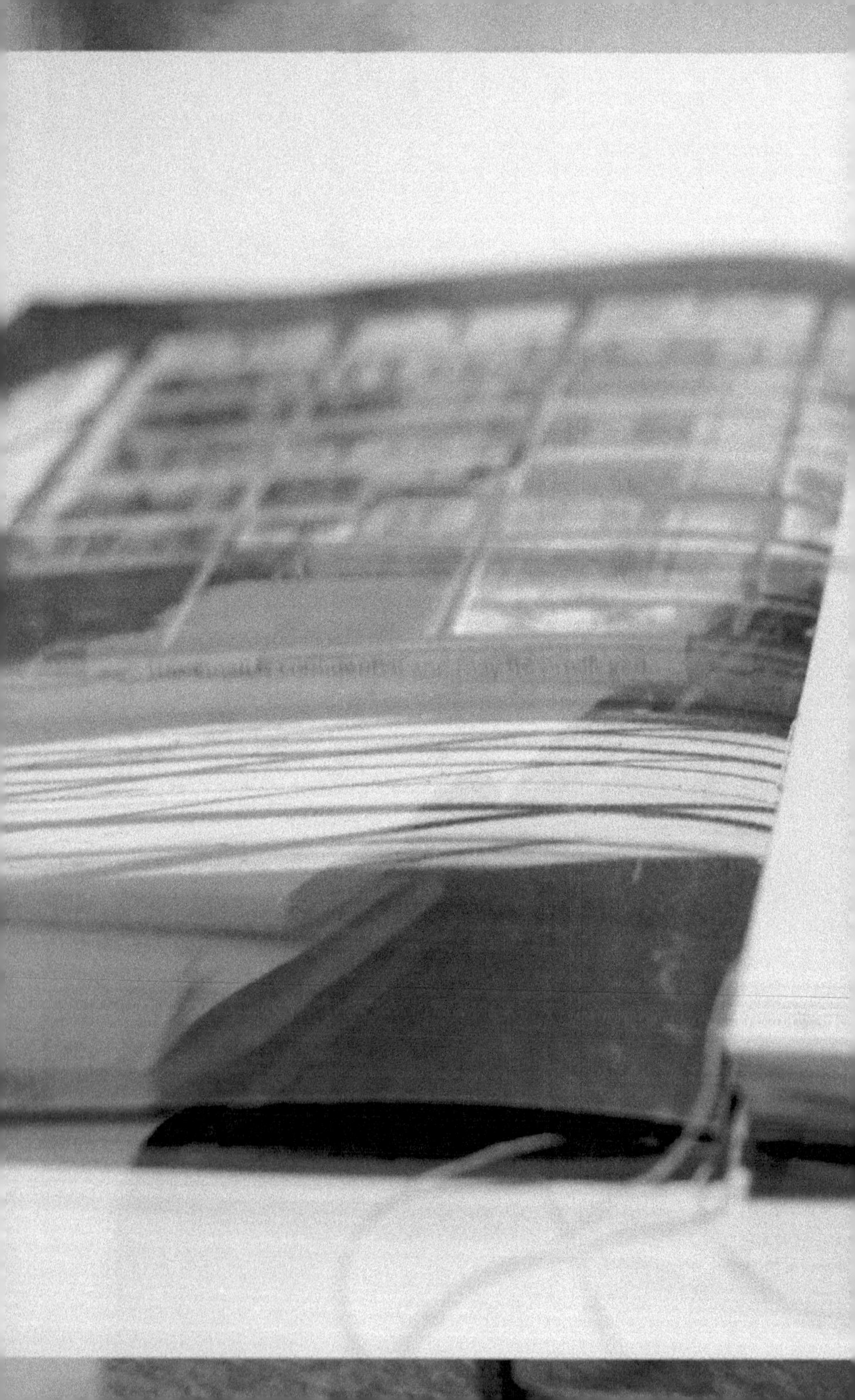

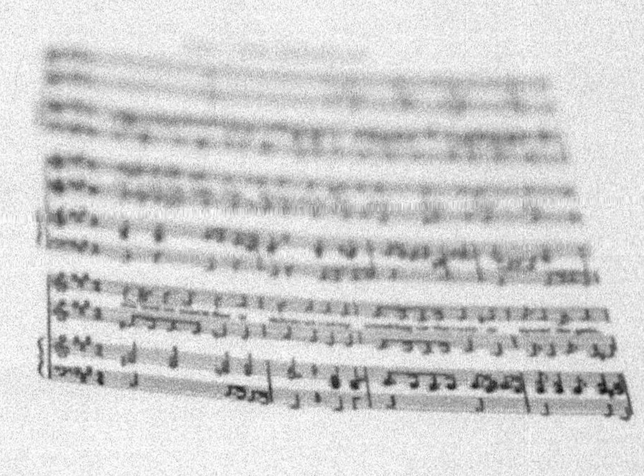

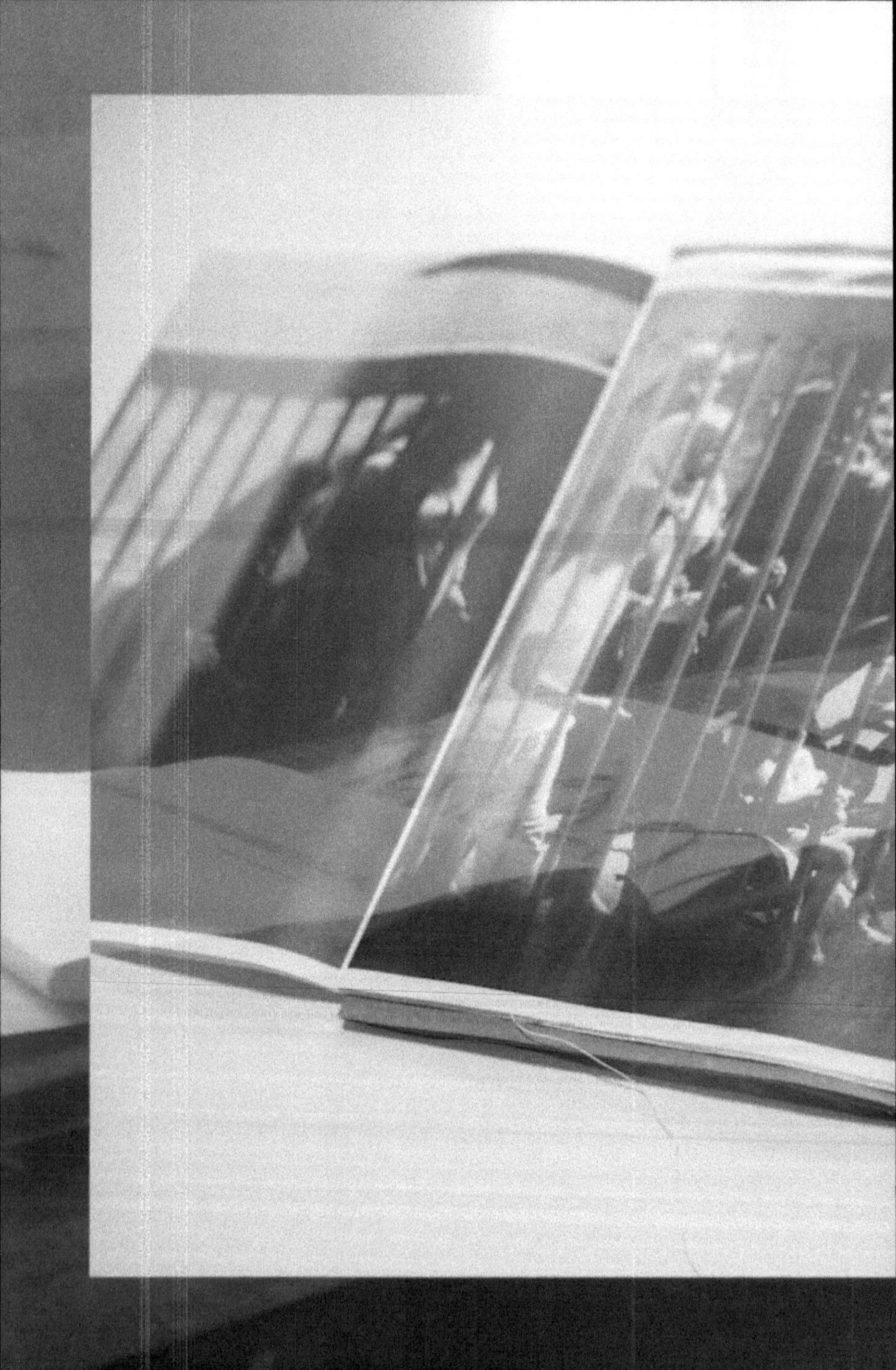

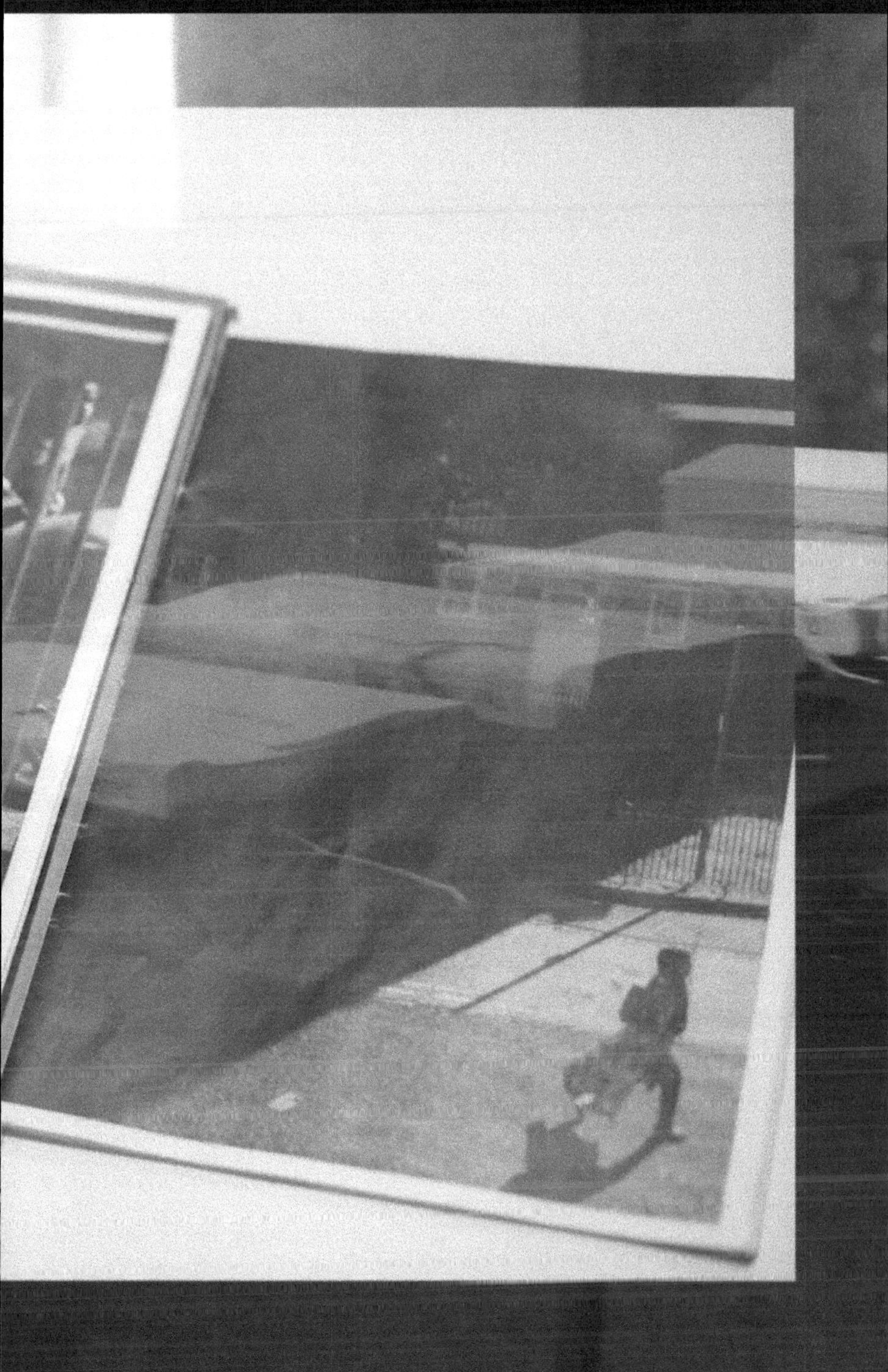

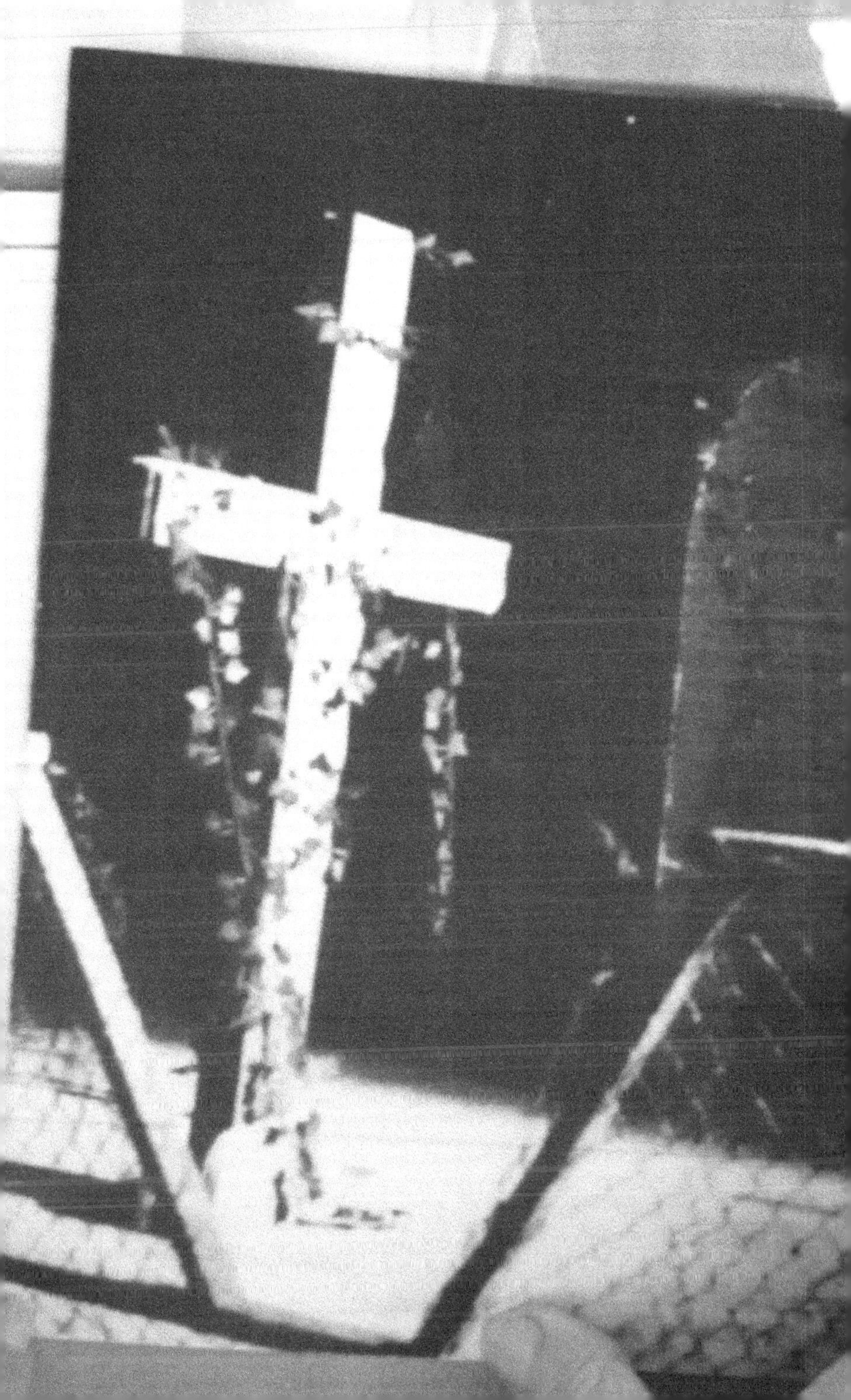

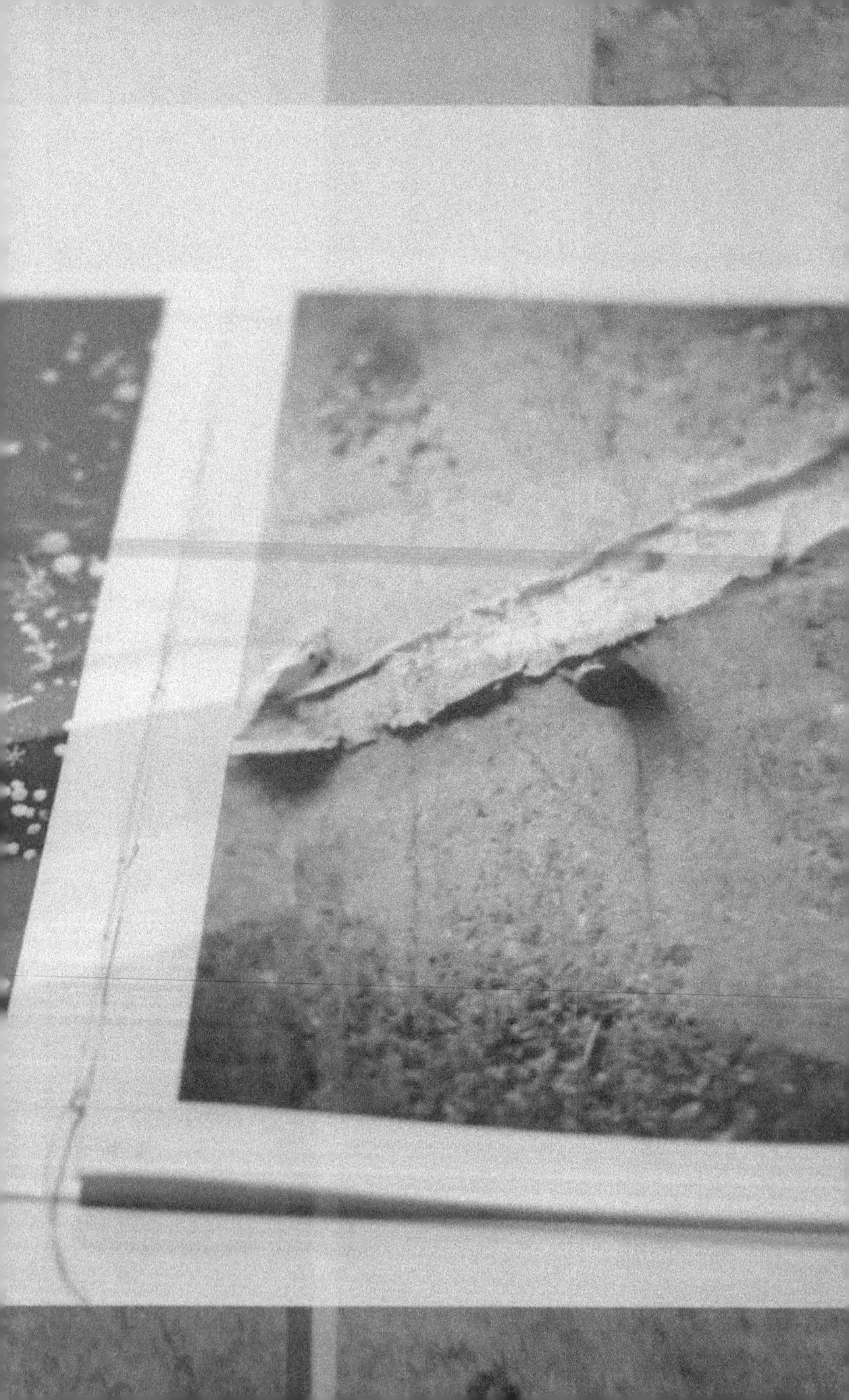

3. Museography of the artist's studio: the artist's museum

This chapter analyses whether the term 'museography' is applicable to paula's practice, and what are the precise contours of this 'museography' in the activity that paula exercises in her live, work and exhibiting spaces, which she calls house–studio–galleries.

This investigation into the musealisation of paula's studio started in the two previous chapters with the notions of spatio–temporal sequencing in the space of the building, and paula's live–work method, a triple 'dispositif' which I designated as 'immersion.'

It is further explored in this chapter in relation to the concept of 'museography' and Kettle's Yard house–museum, a museum model I investigate in reference to paula's house–studio–gallery; and, finally, with the applicability of the notion of 'artist's museum' to her space.

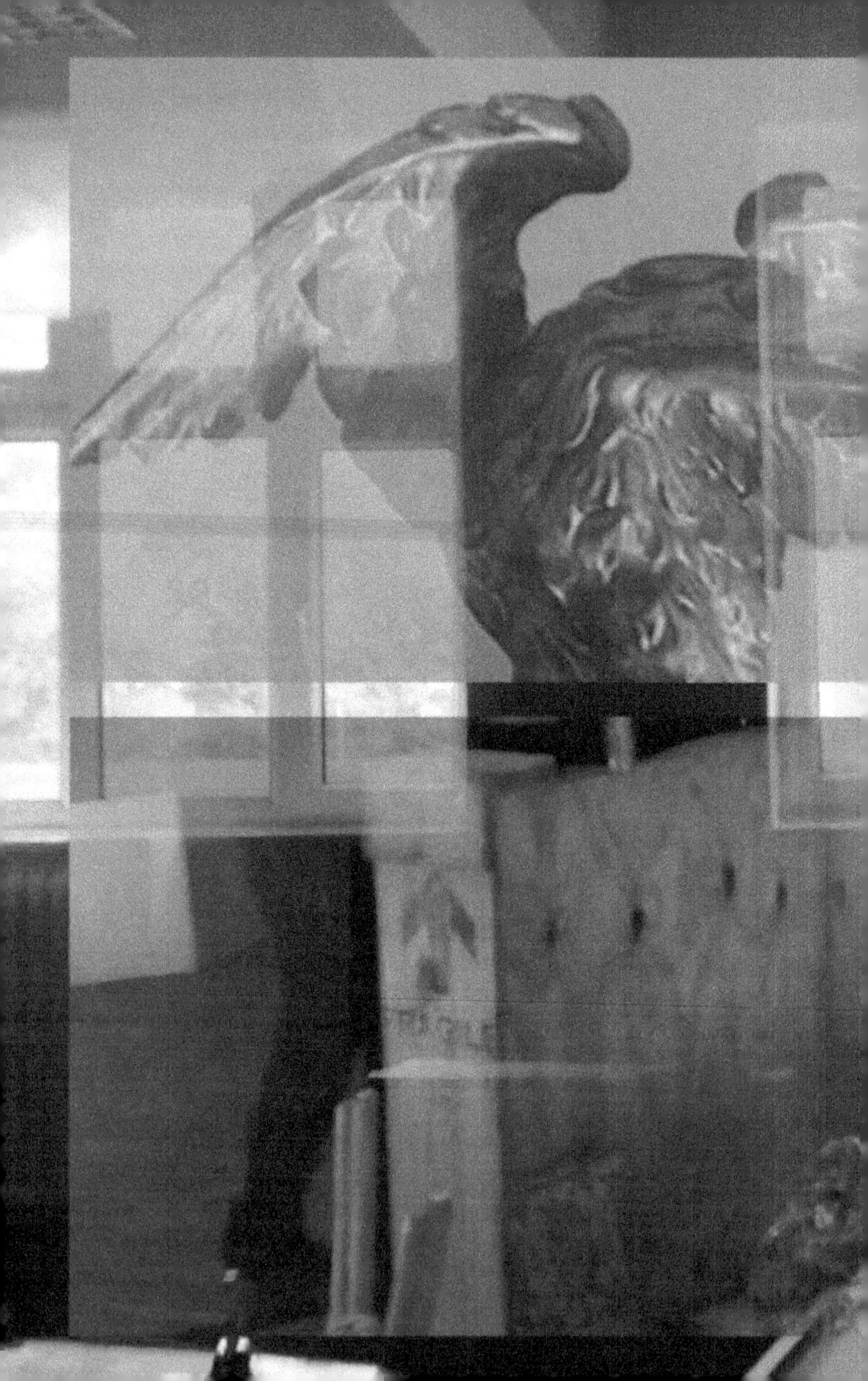

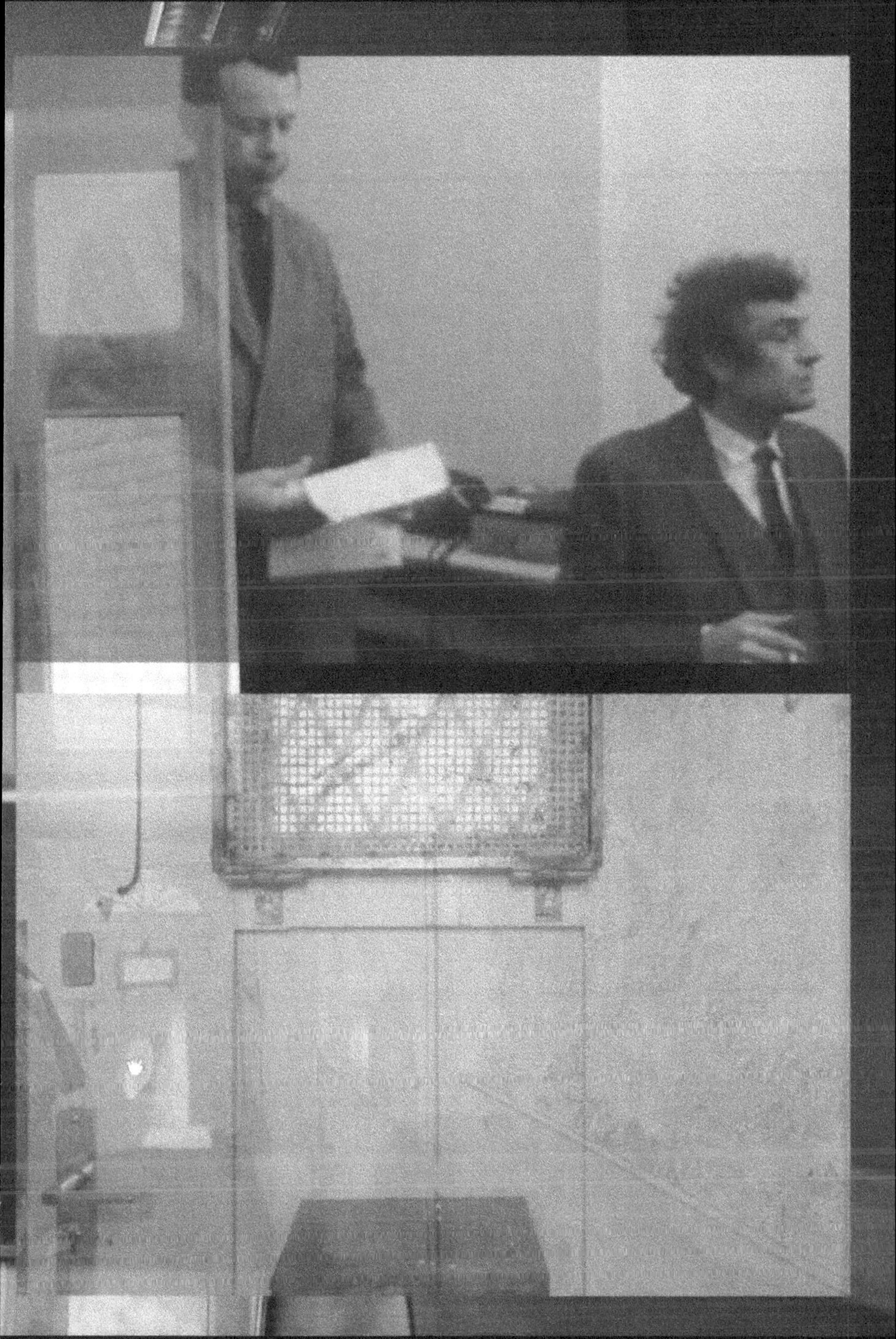

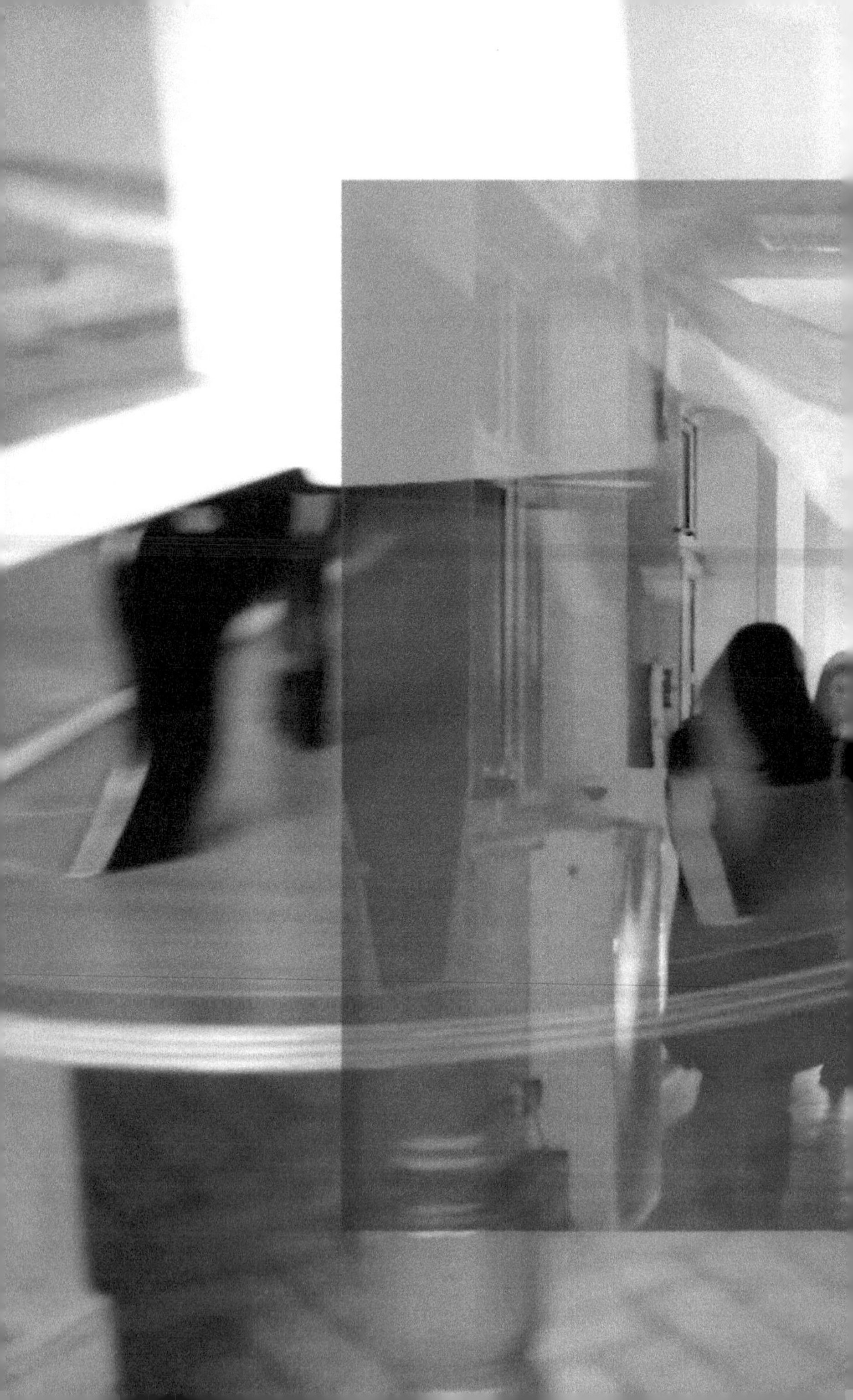

Museography

I am interested in understanding the extent to which paula's spatial activity comprises a 'museographic program' and whether paula, like a 'museographer,' executes it as André Desvallées and François Mairesse define it:

> *More generally, what we call the 'museographic program' encompasses the definition of the contents of the exhibition and its imperatives, as well as the set of functional relationships between the exhibition spaces and the other spaces of the museum. This definition does not imply that museography is limited to the*

visible aspects of the museum. The museographer, as a museum professional, takes into account the requirements of the scientific and management program of the collections, and seeks an adequate presentation of the objects selected by the conservator. S/he knows the methods of conservation or inventory of the museum objects. S/he elaborates a scenography based on the contents, proposes a discursive construction that includes complementary mediations that can help understanding, in addition to being concerned with the demands of audiences, mobilising communication techniques adapted to the good reception of messages.[31]

31 André Desvallées and François Mairesse (Eds), *Conceitos-chave de Museologia*, (São Paulo: ICOM, 2013), 60. Translation by the author.

This possibility of artists being able to constitute their studios into museographic spaces is of particular relevance for its potential benefits. Artists may dispense with the institutional art circuit, escaping all associated premises and conditions such as need for validation, subjection to the mercantilist logic of the art market, exposure to institutional criticism, acceptance of 'suggestions' from gallery owners and curators and, finally, loss of control over the conditions of production and exhibition of their work.

Short—circuiting all these conditions, by museographing their studios, artists are thus giving their work institutional (museal) status, transforming their production into 'musealia,' that is, into a 'museum object' that integrates the museological field.[32]

The artists' total control over the way their work is exhibited, communicated and preserved — three activities that are part of the museographic process — offers original formats and non–standardised approaches, perfectly adjusted to artists' life style, work and identity.

Devallées and Mairesse write: *"According to common sense, museography designates the becoming of a museum or, more generally, the transformation of a*

32 Desvallées and Mairesse, *Conceitos-chave de Museologia*.

life centre, which can be a centre of human activity or a natural site, into some kind of museum."[33]

This is the first issue we face in applying the term 'museography' to paula's exhibition practice, since her spaces are not museums nor are they expected to be. It is also a question of whether paula's live–work–exhibition process fulfils all the characteristics of the museographic process, as stated by Teresa Azevedo:

> *As a scientific process, museography necessarily comprises the set of museum activities: a work of preservation (selection, acquisition, management, conservation),*

33 Ibid.

research (and therefore cataloguing) and communication (through exhibition, publications, etc.).[34]

Can we identify in paula's activity the work of preservation, research and communication inherent to the museographic activity and, if so, in what way do these specific forms function in paula's artistic practice?

Let us highlight the consequences that the museographic process creates in relation to the objects subject to it. Let's consider what Teresa Azevedo writes on this matter:

34 Teresa Azevedo, *Do ateliê para o museu. Interseções e articulações entre o espaço de criação e o espaço de exposição*, Tese de doutoramento, (Faculdade de Letras, Universidade do Porto: Porto, 2018), 56-58. Translation by the author.

*In fact, any museographic
process necessarily implies
a change in the status of
the museographed object.
According to the definition
proposed by ICOM as one of
the key concepts of museology,
museography designates
"becoming a museum or, more
generally, the transformation
of a life centre, which can be
a centre of human activity or
a natural site, in some type of
museum," characterised by
the "extraction, physical and
conceptual, of something
from its natural or cultural
environment of origin …
transforming it … into a 'museum
object'." However, museography
does not only simply imply*

*"transferring an object to the
physical limits of a museum …"*
*it also takes place when,
through a change of context
and selection process, the
'thesaurisation' and presentation"*
*operate a change in the status
of the object.*[35]

Do objects change status within
the house–studio–gallery?

Is there a change in context?

Does the physical and conceptual
exclusion of the objects from
their origins, transform them into
'museum objects'?

35 Ibid, 127.

The museographic process of artists' studios, is considered by some an anomalous process, as suggested by Azevedo:

> *Although the museography of artists' studios is one of the most obvious types of integration of the studio into the museum, it is far from being a simple and consensual practice. In fact, it raises many questions about the status, role and effective utility of the studio in the museological context (Vincent, 2011); there are several approaches proposed and / or critiqued in the theoretical reflection on this practice, which in turn contributes to the richness of the discussion on the topic. Barbara Dawson, for example, says that*

any project of musealisation of artists' studios tends to reveal the greatest difficulties inherent in their own realisation, which are mainly related to the way in which a private space can be transformed into a public exhibition space: "The studio is an artist's personal enclave where raw materials, instead of complete works, dominate. How can this be presented?" (Cappock, 2005). Daniel F. Herrmann, in turn, is sceptical about the definitive transposition of an artist's studio to a museum, even referring that this process is an anomaly.[36]

In fact, paula's spaces reflect the process of transforming

36 Ibid, 126.

a private space into a public
space, since in her case there
is no clear separation between
spaces dedicated to daily life and
exhibition spaces, and neither is
there a separation between studio
space and exhibition space,
so it is not clear which materials
are 'raw materials' or form
'complete works.'

Add to this the constant
recombination of exhibited
artefacts, whose materials
are constantly moved
around between 'collections'
[agglomerations of materials
or 'sandwiches of materials,'
personal archives (classified by
place and date)] and books,
and vice versa.

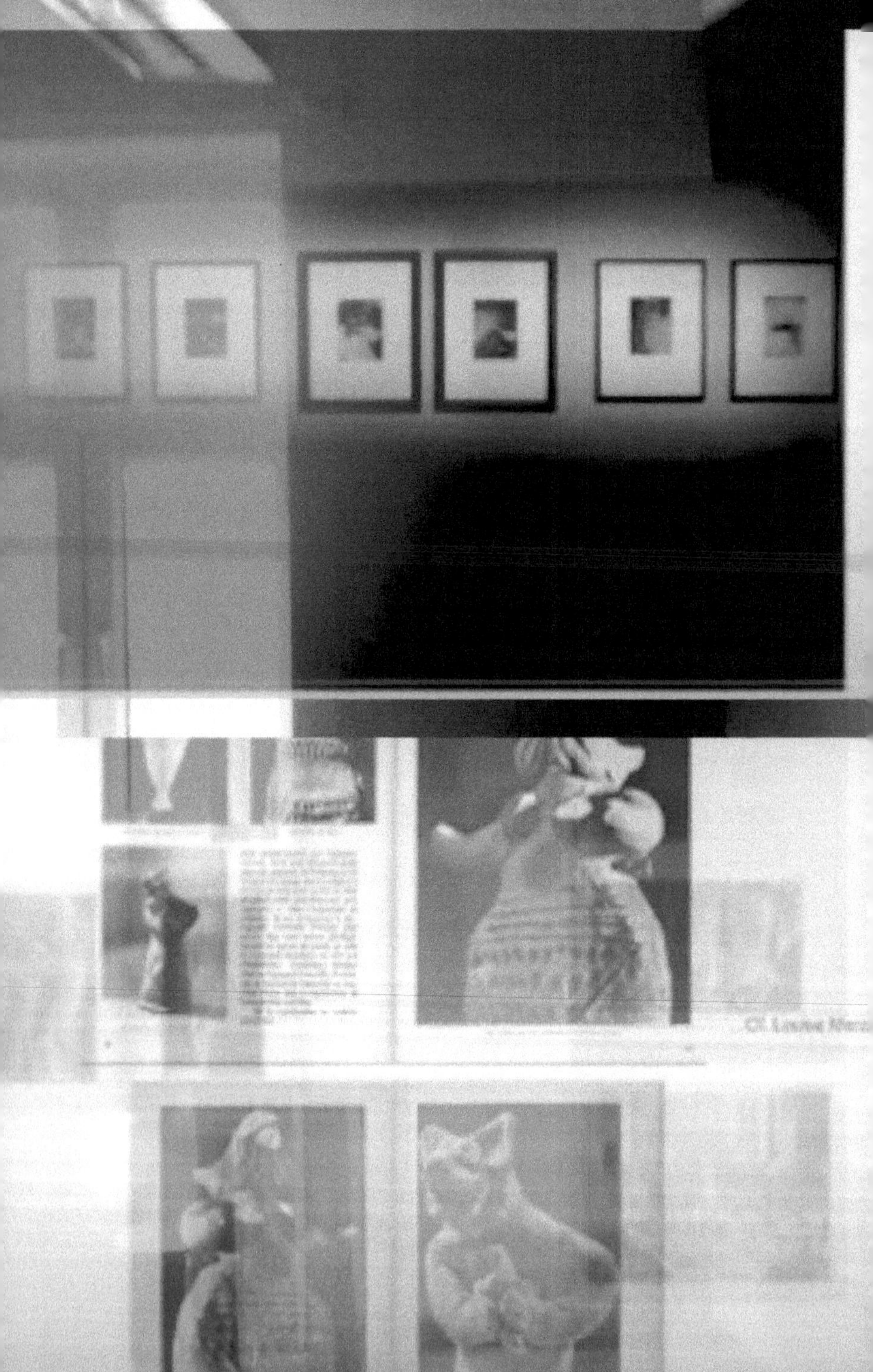

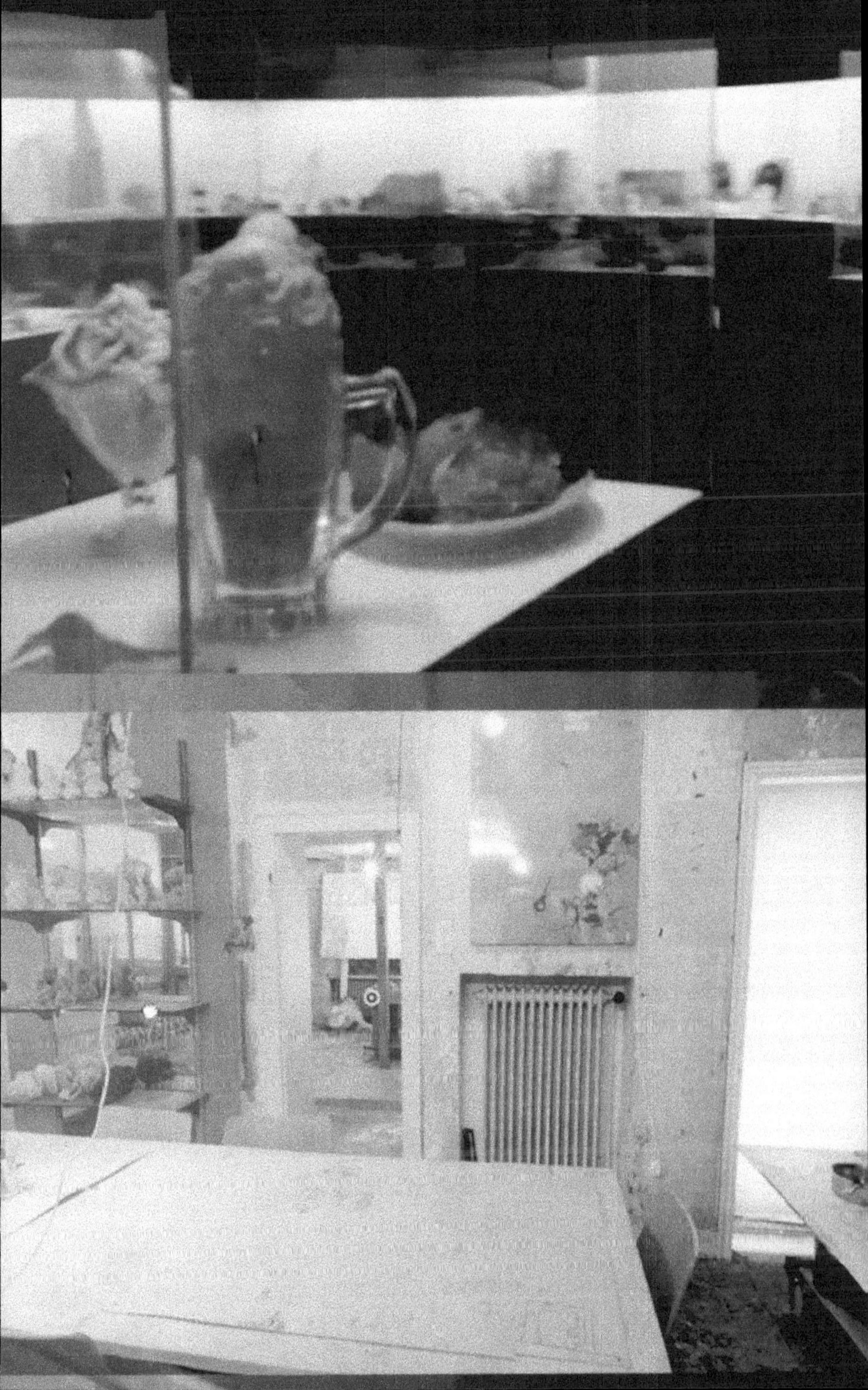

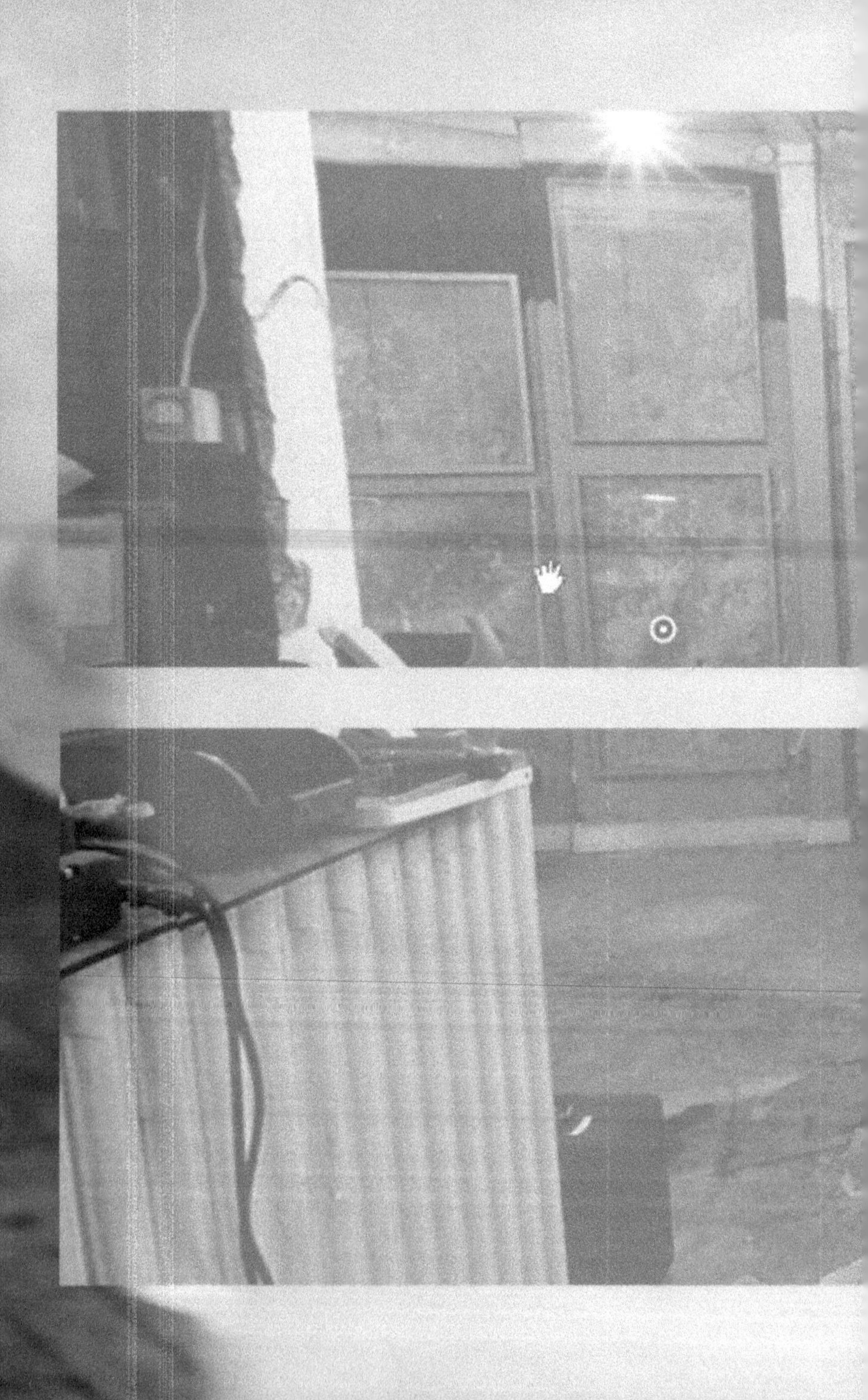

Kettle's Yard

Kettle's Yard is a house-museum, and in 2018 it was the object of an architectural intervention that, whilst preserving the house in the exact conditions in which Jim Ede, its co-creator, left it, endowed it with new spaces, including a floor dedicated to educational programs, an improved gallery (of the *white cube*' typology, built in 1970), a cafeteria and a new entrance to the museum.

The museum has a regular program of contemporary art exhibitions, musical performances, workshops and a program of talks by artists and curators about art, media and archives.

Its website includes documentation of these conversations, related exhibitions, as well as the museum's collection database.

The house–museum was created in 1956 by Jim Ede and his wife Helen Ede as a result of their search for: *"a living space where works of art could be enjoyed … where young people could be at home unhampered by the greater austerity of the museum or public art gallery."*[37] Also, according to the museum's page, in 1966 Jim Ede donated the house and its contents to the University of Cambridge.

37 kettlesyard.co.uk/collection/history/(acedido em 8 de Janeiro 2020)

Jim Ede and Helen Ede lived in Kettle's Yard between 1958 and 1973. Jim was a curator at the Tate Gallery in London in the 1920s and 1930s. It was thanks to his friendships in the art world that he brought together an admirable collection of modern British art, as well as works by foreign artists, including Joan Miró and Constantin Brancusi.

In the house, Jim carefully positioned these works of art alongside furniture, crystals, ceramics and natural elements, trying to create a harmonious whole. His vision of what would become a museological space did not include:

An art gallery or museum, nor
... simply a collection of works
of art reflecting my taste or
the taste of a given period. It
is, rather, a continuing way of
life from these last fifty years,
in which stray objects, stones,
glass, pictures, sculpture, in light
and in space, have been used to
make manifest the underlying
stability.[38]

That is, Kettle's Yard in its origin was — and still is, since this didn't change — an exhibition space in a domestic environment open to the public and without ever ceasing to be a live–work space for Jim and Helen, which is identical to what happens in paula's house–studio–gallery.

38 ibid.

However, the existence of the studio in paula's space, creates an important distinction in relation to Jim and Helen's house–museum space and the studio–museum, a distinction that we can perhaps characterise as Azevedo does:

> *House–museums are distinct from studio–museums in that in the latter it is the work space itself that justifies and is at the origin of the musealisation process, and it is this space that guides all the definition, activities and programming of the space.*[39]

Let's examine whether paula's house–studio–gallery also fits the current definition of a museum,

39 Azevedo, *Do ateliê para o museu*, 129.

mentioned by Devallées and Mairesse:

> *The professional definition of a museum best known today remains the one found in the statutes of the International Council of Museums (ICOM), 2007: "The museum is a permanent, non-profit institution, serving society and its development, open to the public, which acquires, preserves, studies, exhibits and transmits the material and immaterial heritage of humanity and its environment, for the purposes of study, education and delight."[40]*

40 Desvallées and Mairesse, *Conceitos-chave de Museologia*, 64.

The attributes of this definition
are fully met by Kettle's Yard in
its current version. However,
paula's house–studio–gallery has
particularities that differentiate it
from the concepts and methods
normalised in the activities
of institutionalised museums,
namely:

It is not an institution;

It carries out activities that are
not always for profit, such as
exhibitions and collaborative
research, without disregard
however, for the commercial value
and sale of its artistic production
(installations and publications);

It is not, exactly, at the service
of society because it aims at
a very segmented public (as

happened with Kettle's Yard in the beginning);

If it transmits the material and immaterial heritage of its environment, it only does so within the scope of its projects and within the scope of the immersive process (paula's live–work method) that we have already described.

The same applies to its objects of "study, education and delight."

In other words, they are all activities of a personal nature, which are not intended to address the general public, without distinction, which is the primary condition of a museum.

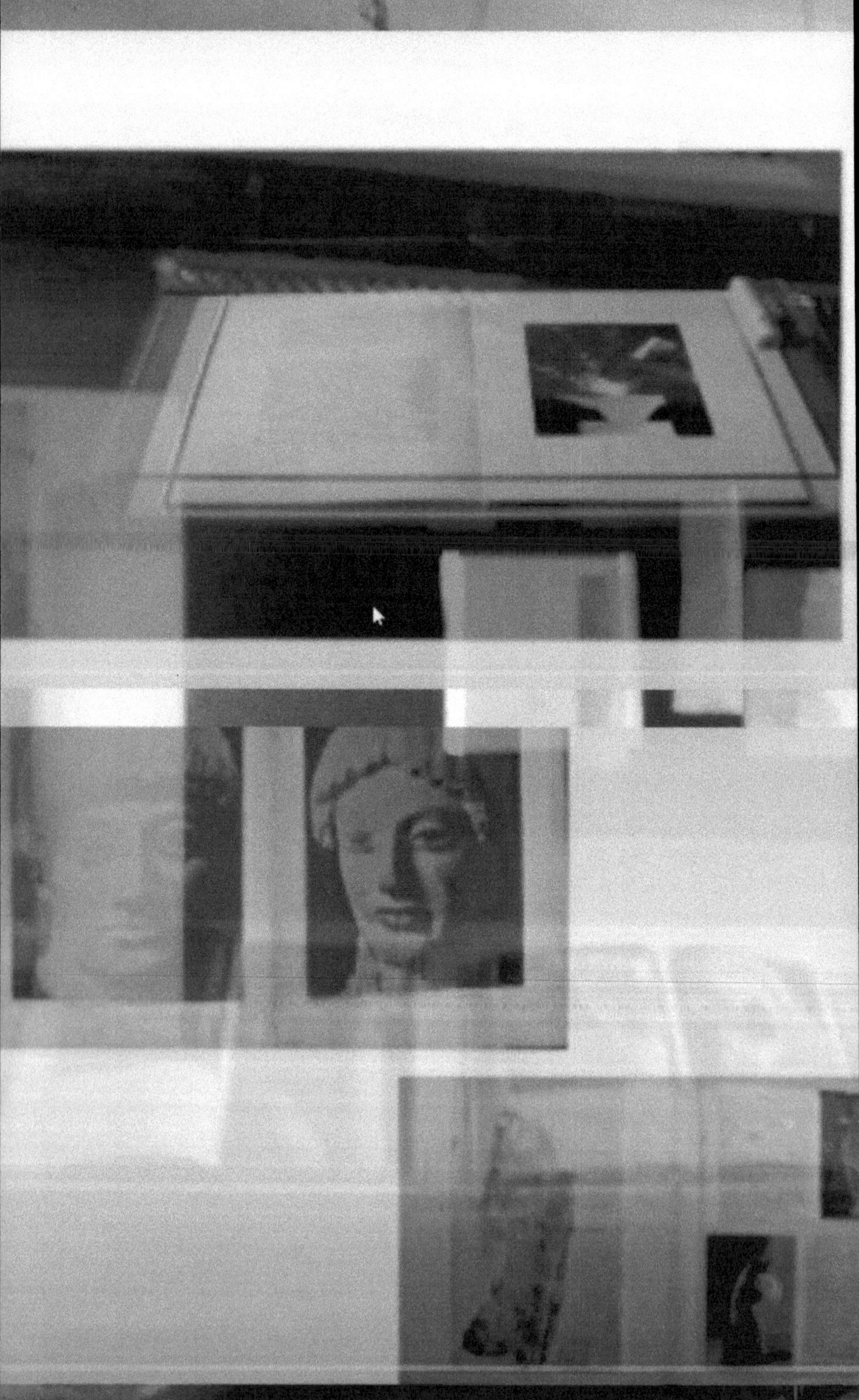

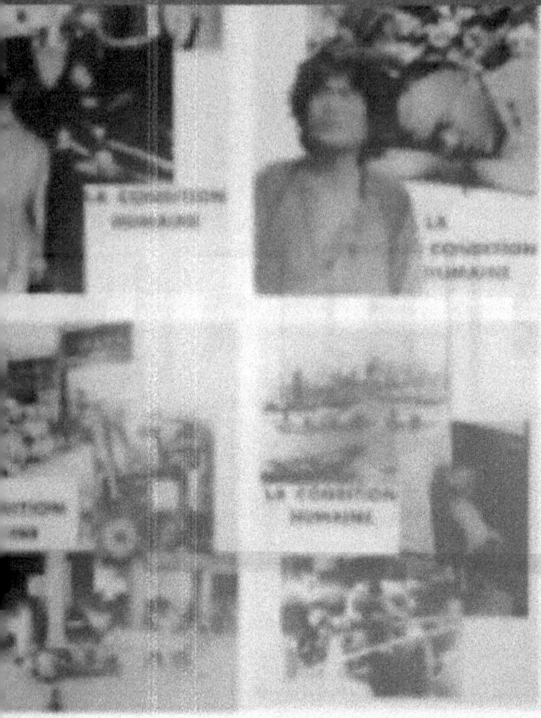

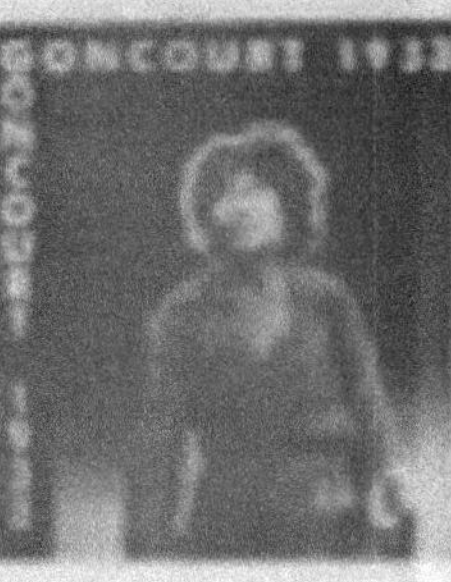
André Malraux
La condition
humaine
GONCOURT 1933

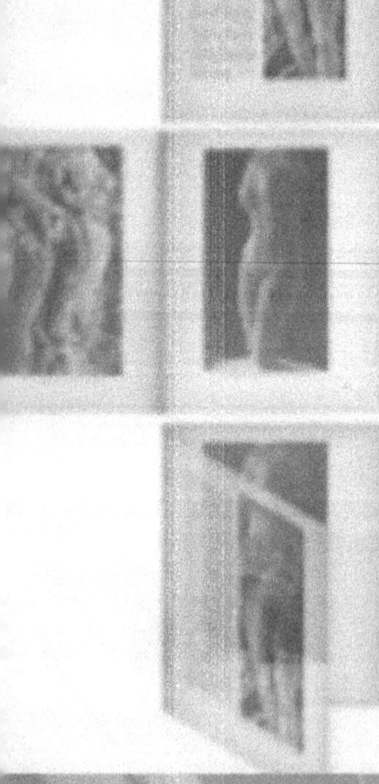

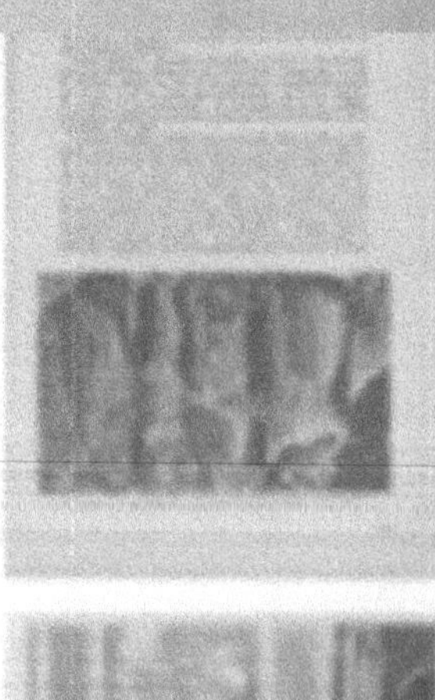

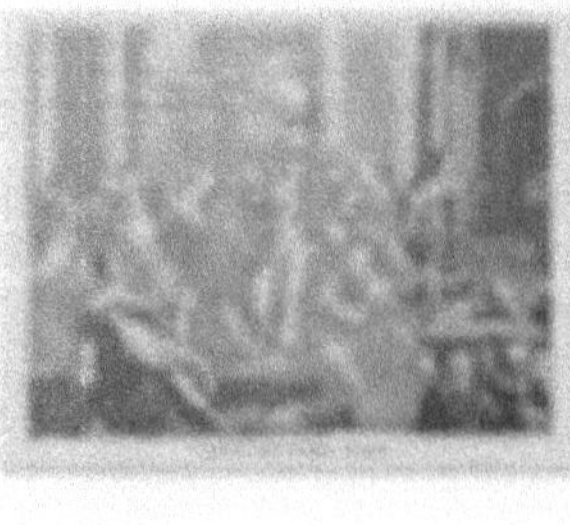

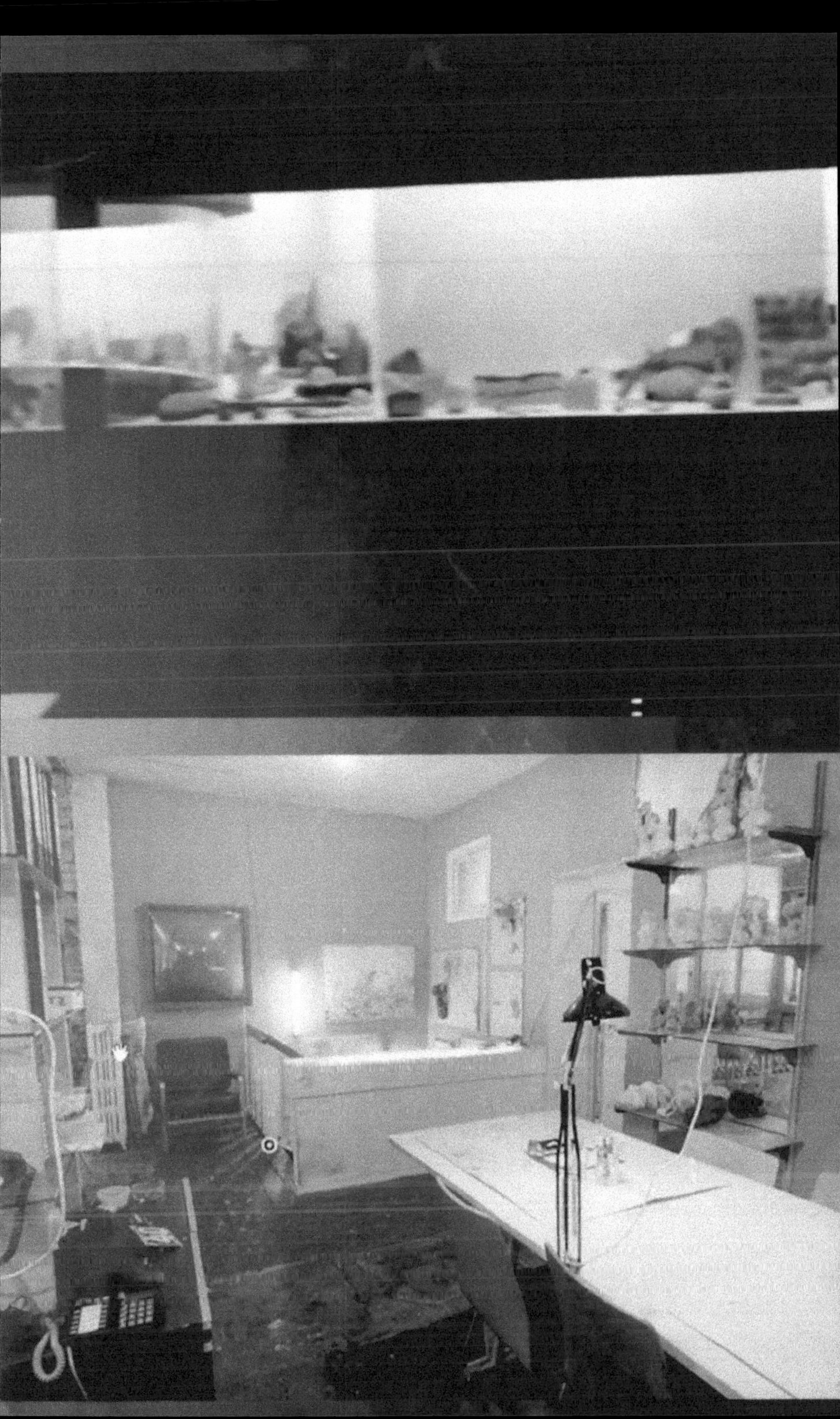

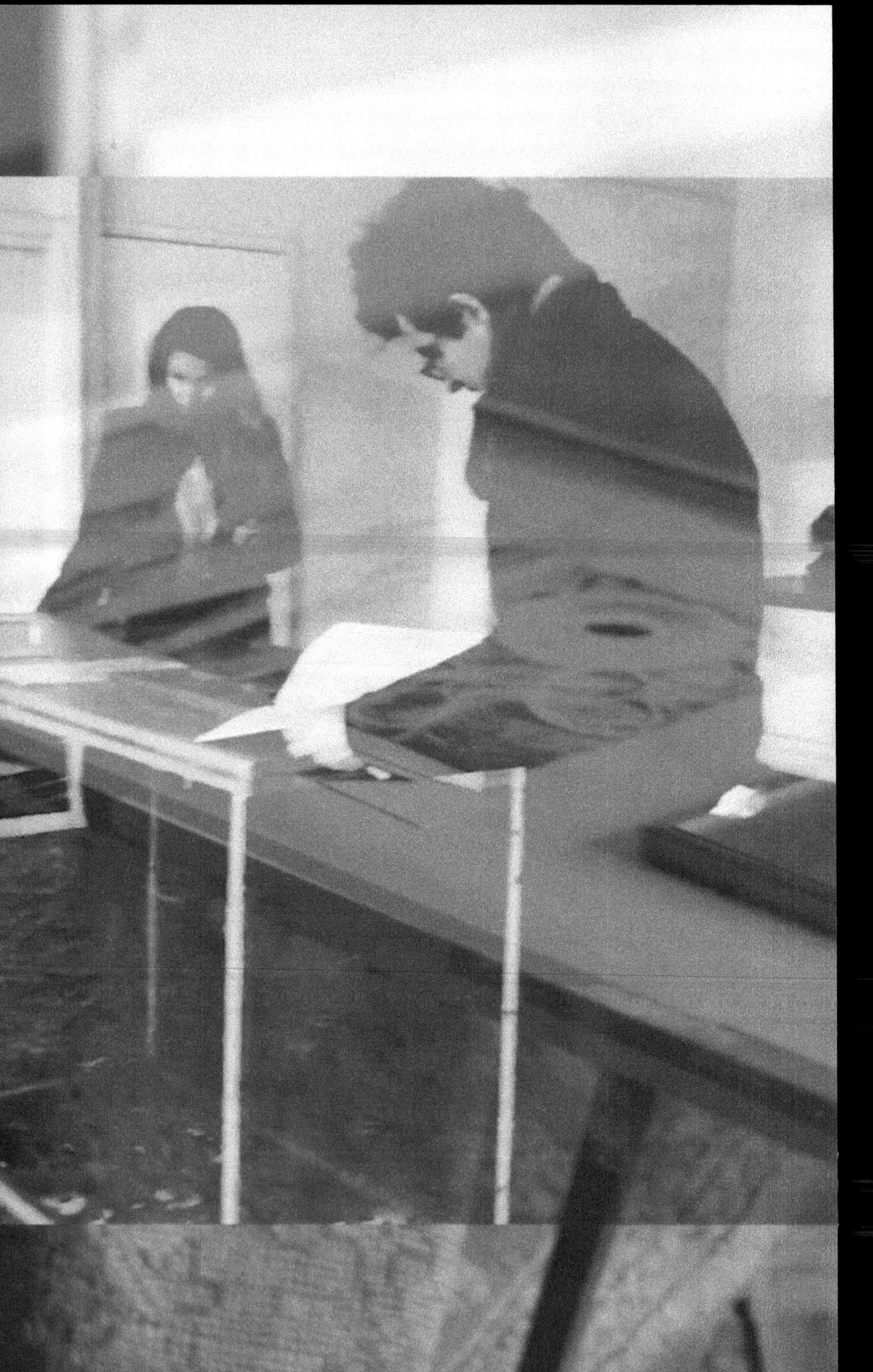

The artist's museum

The musealisation of paula's house–studio–gallery can be contextualised by the critique of the contemporary art museum and its functions that emerged in the 1960s. Let's see what Elisa de Noronha Nascimento says about this:

> *In the meanwhile, what is perceived as a distinct reaction, typical of this second phase of the contemporary art museum, are the strategies that many artists have found / find to problematise museological structures and discourses. Two of these strategies we choose to highlight are: the appropriation of the museological language —*

the collection, the catalogue, the inventory, the exhibition — and the unveiling of its discursive structures as artistic poetics.[41]

In this consideration of what are the main functions of the museum — collecting, cataloguing, investigating and exhibiting — we can find a theoretical and practical framework for paula's idiosyncratic and specific activities, translated in exhibitions (which she curates in her space with her own works and those by other artists), in the collections (gleaning of materials from the surrounding vicinity and their organization in material constellations) and, finally, in the

41 Elisa de Noronho Nascimento, *Discursos e reflexividade: um estudo sobre a musealização da arte contemporânea*, Tese de doutoramento, (Universidade do Porto: Porto, 2013), 138-139. Translation by the author.

inventory and cataloguing of the projects that paula elaborates and makes available on her website.

The same is true with her catalogues, with the elaboration and printing of her publications and with the formation of her *ad hoc* archives. paula's house–studio–gallery fits neatly within another type of museum space, such as the artist's museum. Let us refer, again, to Nascimento's writing :

In this context, two exhibitions stand out: the 5th Kassel Documenta, held in 1972 and curated by Harald Szeemann (1933-2005), where for the first time Szeemann will use the term artist's museum, referring to the relationship between artistic creation and the principle of museum administration, presenting museum models and fictions such as the 'Mouse Museum' (1965-1977) by Claes Oldenburg (b.1929), the 'Bôite-en-valise' (1935-1941) by Marcel Duchamp, and the 'Museum of Modern Art, Department of Eagles' (1968-1971) by Marcel Broodthaers (1924-1976).[42]

We witness, therefore, in paula's case, another type of space that presents itself as a museum space, as an alternative to the modern institutional museum.

42 Ibid, 140.

On that topic, write Devallées and Mairesse:

The museal establishment is a concrete form of museal institution. We can see that the institution's contestation, or its pure and simple denial (as in the case of the imaginary museum of Malraux [1947] or the fictional museum of the artist Marcel Broodthaers), does not result in a break with the museal field, insofar as this can be conceived outside the institutional framework (in its strictest sense, the expression 'virtual museum,' or 'potential museum' —which exists in essence, but not in fact —accounts for these museal experiences at the margins of the institutional reality).[43]

It is undoubtedly in this typology of spaces that we find paula's house—studio—gallery and it is in this context that we can argue that her live—work—exhibition space is a museal space.

43 Desvallées and Mairesse, *Conceitos-chave de Museologia*, 51.

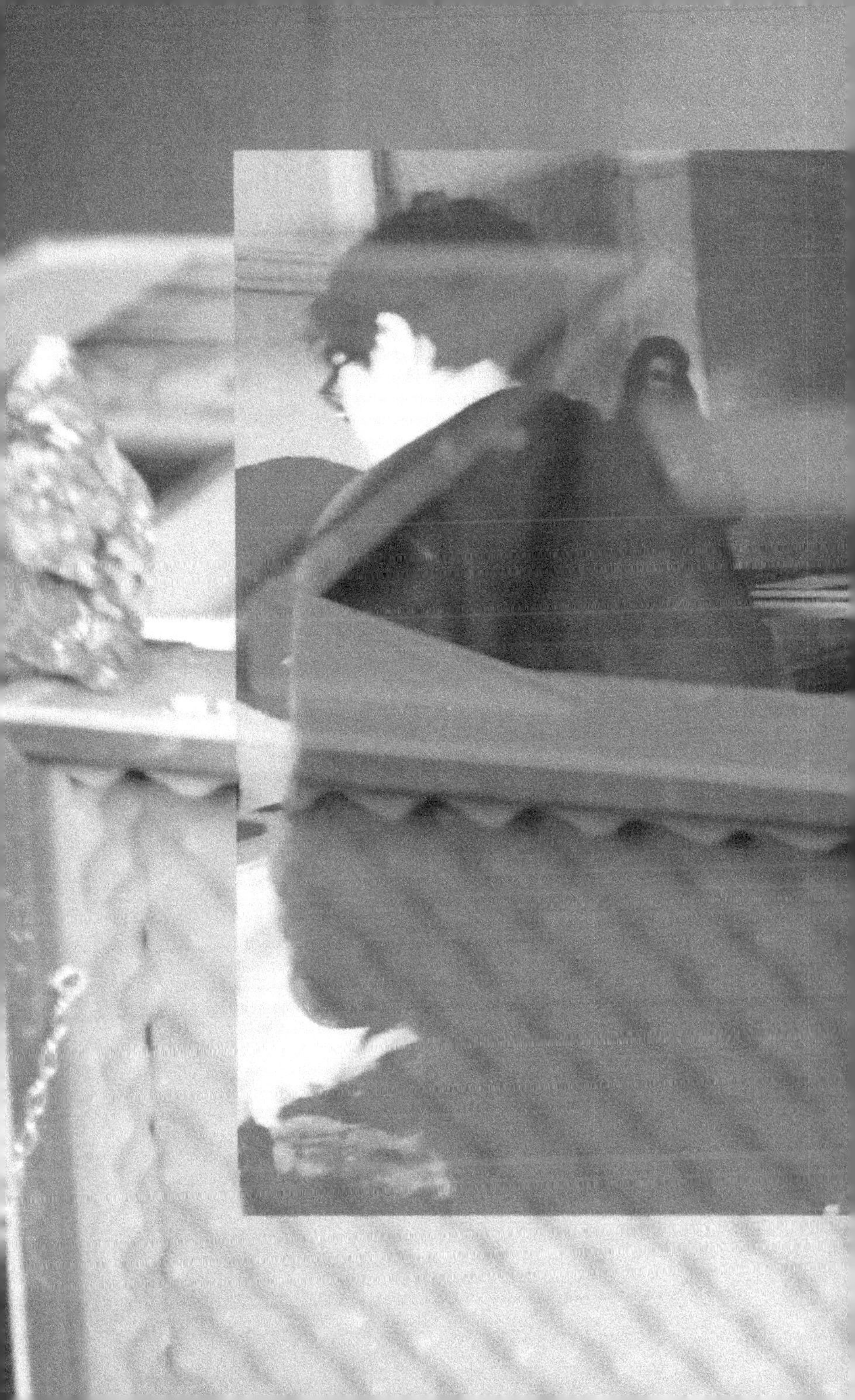

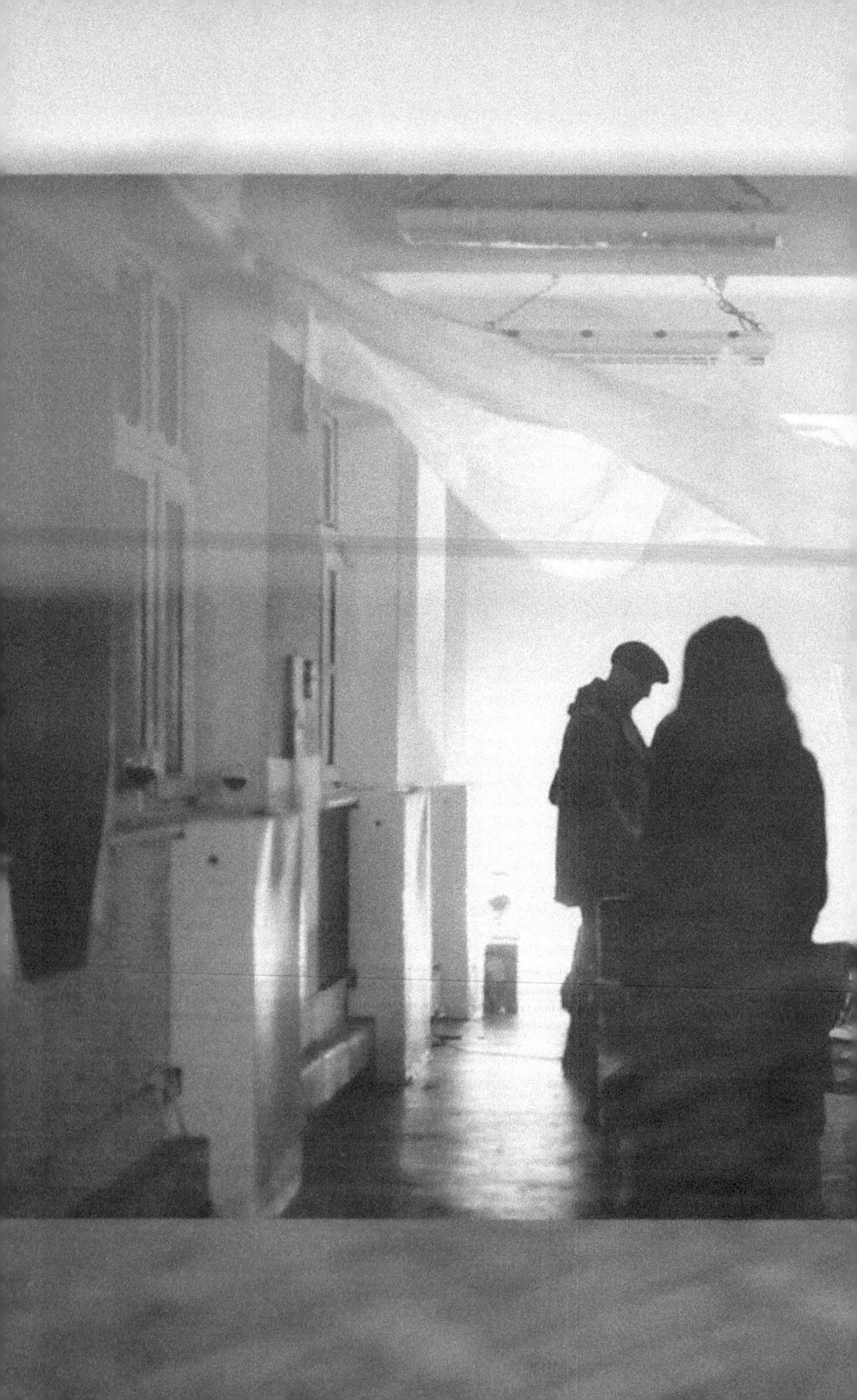

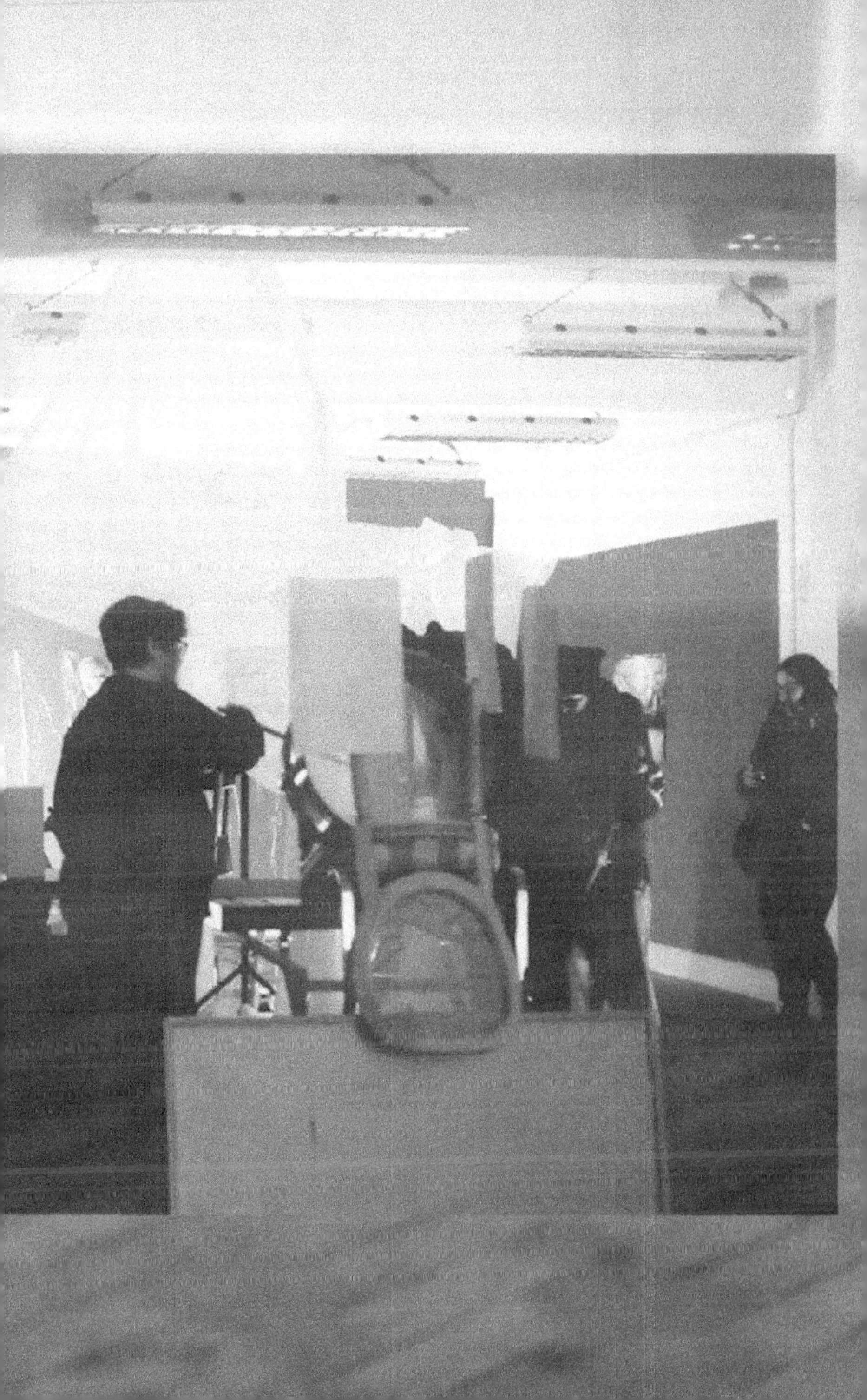

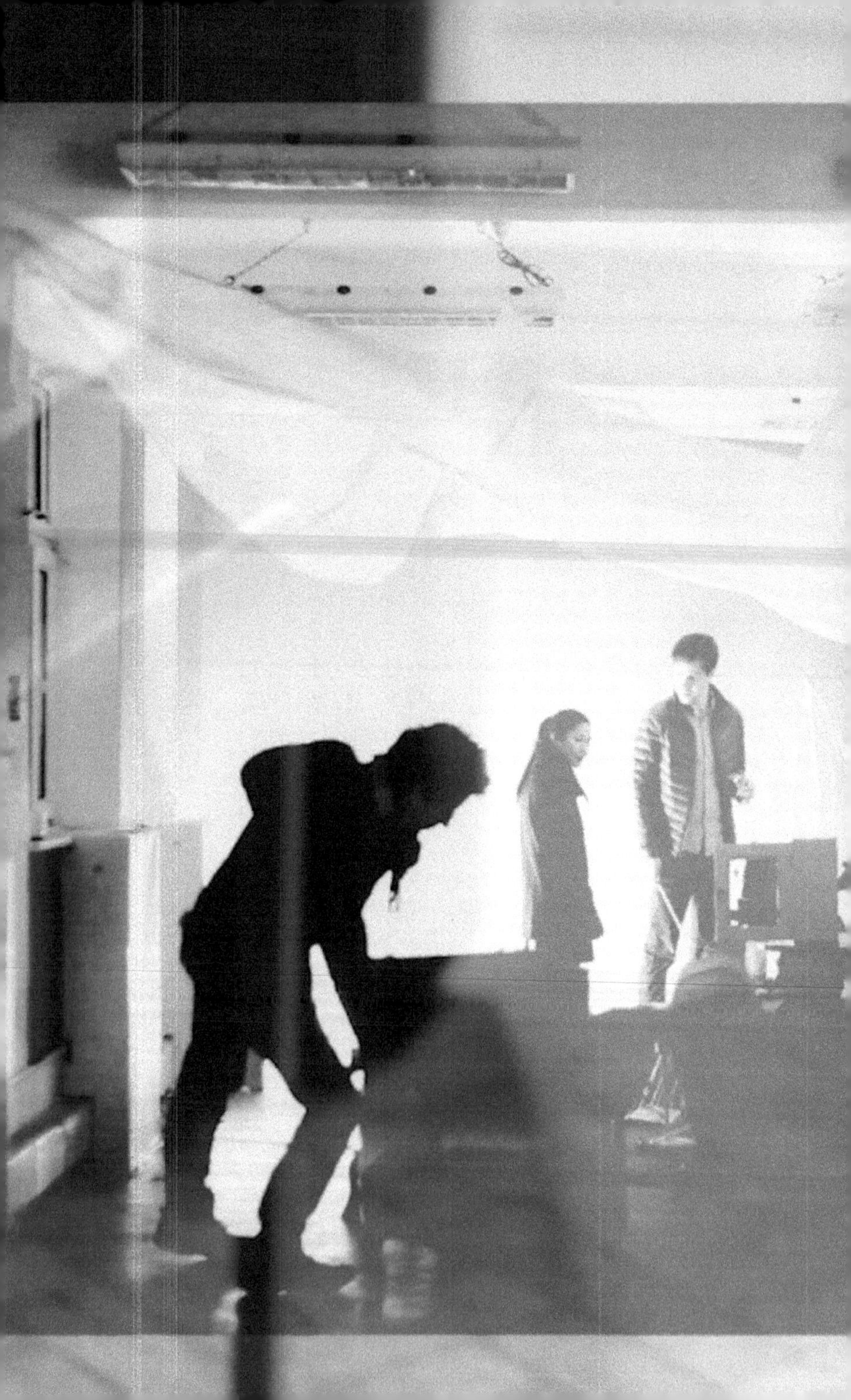

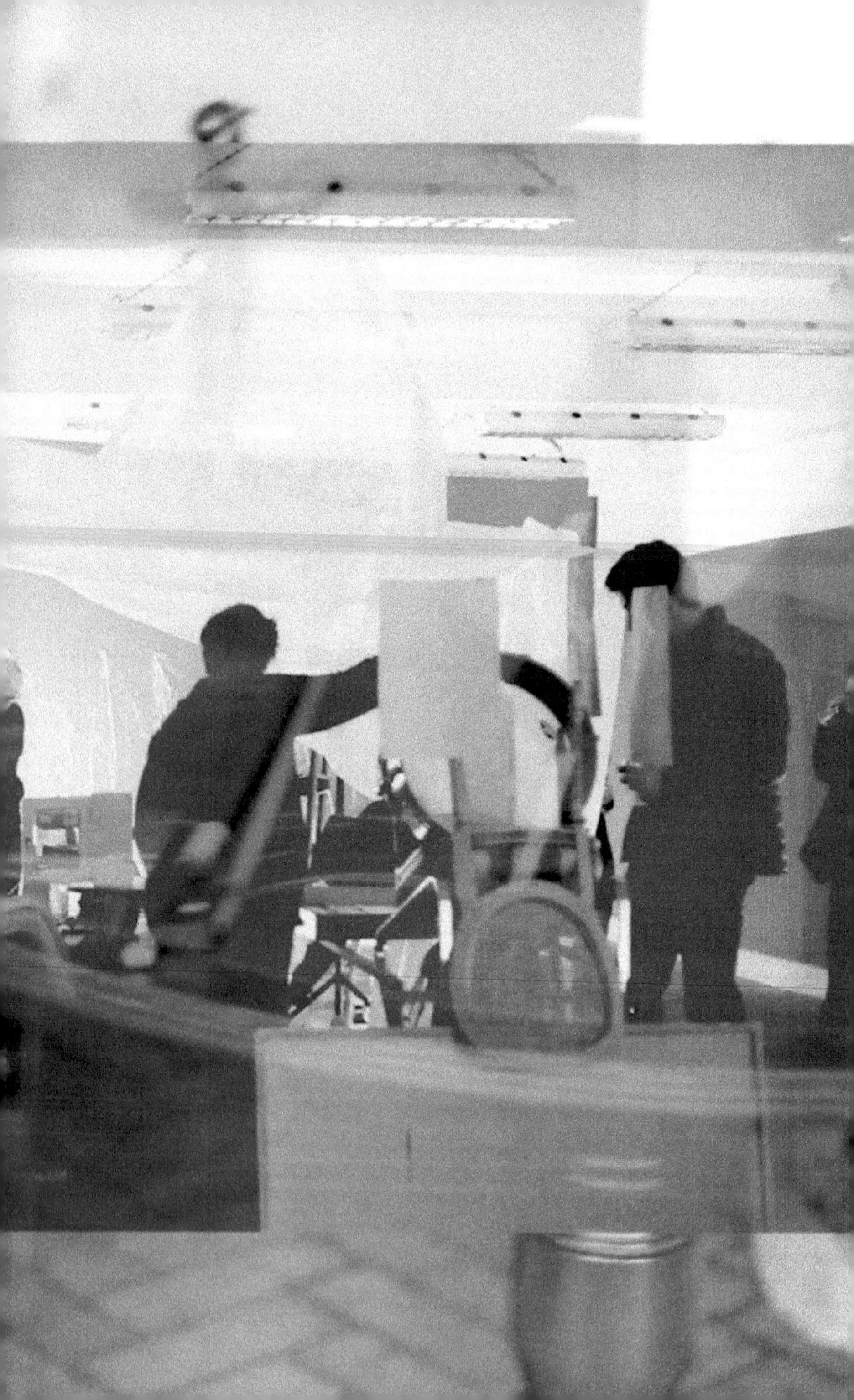

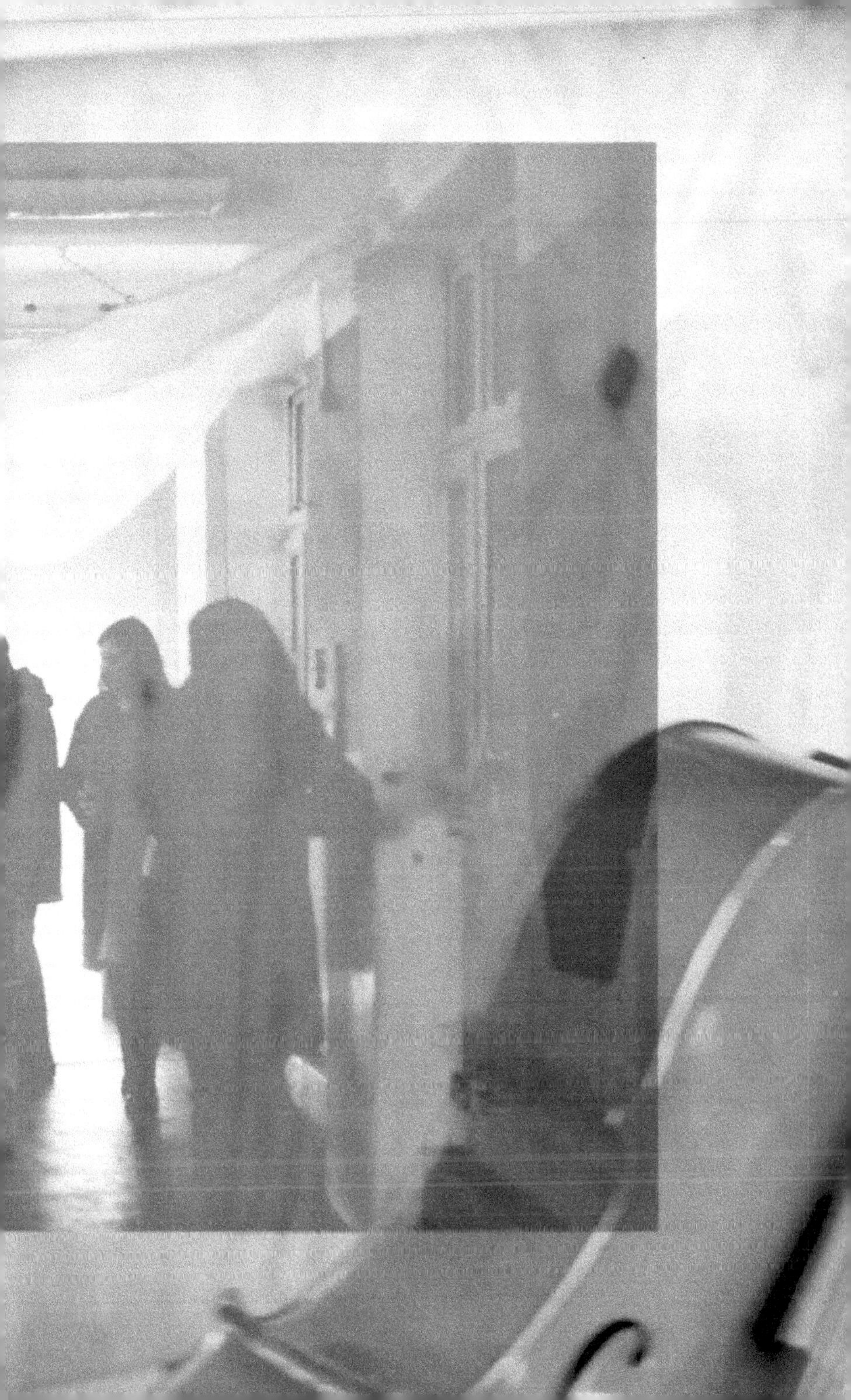

REFERENCES

Adams, Tony E., Ellis, Carolyn and Jones, Stacy Holmes. "Autoethnography." In *The International Encyclopedia of Communication Research Methods*. Hoboken, NJ: John Wiley & Sons, 2017.

Azevedo, Teresa, *Do ateliê para o museu. Interseções e articulações entre o espaço de criação e o espaço de exposição*. Faculdade de Letras, Universidade do Porto: Porto, 2018.

Bader, Barbara, "Books as Collections: Dieter Roth's Artists' Books as Case in Point," in *Journal of the Oxford University History Society*, n.3: 2005.

Crespo, Nuno, "Ser pontual num encontro que só pode falhar. Notas sobre a contemporaneidade do artista," In P. Hussak, ed., *Poiésis, Arte contemporânea: anacronismo e pós-conceitualismo*. Florianopolis: Editora Federal Fluminense, 2016.

Desvallées, André and Mairesse, François, eds, *Conceitos-chave de Museologia*. São Paulo: ICOM, 2013.

Nascimento, Elisa de Noronho, *Discursos e reflexividade: um estudo sobre a musealização da arte contemporânea*, Universidade do Porto: Porto, 2013.

Sardo, Delfim "O Enorme Campo Do Que Não Tem Nome," in *O Exercício Experimental da Liberdade*. Lisboa: Orfeu Negro, 2017.

Rancière, Jacques, *The future of the Image*. London: Verso, 2007.
---. *The emancipated spectator*. London: Verso, 2009.
---. *The future of the Image*. London: Verso, 2007.
---. *O Espectador emancipado*. Lisboa: Orfeu Negro, 2010.

Rockhill, Gabriel, "Appendix I: Glossary of Technical Terms," In Jacques Ranciere, *The Politics of Aesthetics- The Distribution of the Sensible*. London and New York: Bloomsbury Academic, 2013.

LIST OF WORKS

All photographs of artists' books and museums, and exhibitions in this book are from the video-essay *The expanded practice of the artist's book: Immersion in the artist's museum* by Francisco Varela, Video HD, 11m 05", English

_ARTISTS'BOOKS (p. 31-34)

Bodman, Sarah, *The Marsh Test*. VSW, 2002.

Drucker, Johanna, *Narratology*. US: 1994.
---. *The Current Line*. Wisconsin: Druckwerk, 1996.
---. *Prove before Laying: Figuring the Word*. US: Druckwerk, 1997

Holt, Nancy, *Ransacked*. US: Lapp Princess Press, Inc, 1980.

Meador, Clifton, *A.A.A.R.P.US*. US: 1994.
All Retrieved from Artistsbooksonline.org

Knowles,Alison, *The Big Book*, NY: Something Else Gallery, 1967. Retrieved from x-traonline.org, bomdiabooks.de and visible language 26, 1/2

King, Susan E., *Women and Cars.* Rosendale, N.Y.: Women's Studio Workshop; Los Angeles: Paradise Press, 1983. Retrieved from uknow.uky.edu

Smith, Keith A., *Book 91*, Barrytown, NY: Space Heater Multiples, 1982. Retrieved from blogs.getty.edu.

Filliou, Robert, *Sans Objet / Without Object,* 1984. Retrieved from richardsaltoun.com

Ruppersberg, Allen, *The New Five Foot Shelf,* CAAC Collection, 2001. Retrieved from artmap.com.

MacCallum, Marlene, *Corner*, Canada, 2013. Retrieved from marlenemaccallum.com

Matta-Clark, Gordon, *Splitting*, New York: 98 Greene Street Loft Press, 1974.

Ono, Yoko, *Grapefruit*, Tokyo: Wunternaum Press, 1964. Retrieved from MOMA/PS1blog

---. *Dream Come True*. Argentina: MALBA, 2016. Retrieved from Artistsmultiples.blogspot.com

Roth, Dieter, *Literature Sausage (Literaturwurst)*, 1969. Retrieved from MOMA.org

_ARTISTS' MUSEUMS (p. 140-169)

Dieter Roth, *Schimmelmuseum 1992-2004*. Retrieved from dieterrothmuseum.org

Claes Oldenburg, *Mouse Museum, 1965-77*. Retrieved from artdone.

André Malraux, *Le Musée Imaginaire*, first dummy, 1947. Retrieved from Mouna Mekouar, *L'écran comme nouveau sanctuaire: Malraux et le Musée Imaginaire*, La Source du Lion, 2017.

Marcel Broodthaers, *Musée d'Art Moderne, Département des Aigles, Section XIXème Siècle*, Brussels, 1968. Retrieved from FR3 (Collection: Les arts).

_EXHIBITIONS (throughout the book)

Undisclosed Location: paula roush Teresa Paiva Zeigam Azizov Whitechapel London, February 2016

Evidencing The East End: paula roush Julie Cook Whitechapel London, May 2016

Domenest: paula roush Natércia Caneira Woolwich London, December 2019—June 2020.

Special thanks for their contribution to *Domenest* performative installation: David Goldenberg, John Peter Askew, Anila Ladwa, Mary Goodwin, Sarah Doyle, Sarah Anslie, Shannon Ho, Gergo Csomos, Vanja Karas, Richard, Ana Benlloch, George Parnell.

THE EXPANDED PRACTICE OF THE ARTIST'S BOOK:
IMMERSION IN THE ARTIST'S MUSEUM

Essay: Francisco Varela
Design:mobile_strategies
Typeface: Museo by Jos Buivenga

Published on the occasion of
MUSEUMS WITHOUT WALLS
conference+exhibition
curated by: Gabriel Menotti
Isabel Bader Centre Queen's University
Kingston Canada August 15-17 2022

ISBN: 978-1-7390996-9-5

Supported by:
School of Arts and Creative Industries
Centre for the Study of Networked Image
at London South Bank University

msdm publications
www.msdm.org.uk

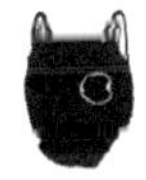